Farmworker's Daughter

Rose Castillo Guilbault

Farmworker's Daughter

GROWING UP
MEXICAN
IN AMERICA

Heyday Books, Berkeley, California

Heyday Books, founded in 1974, works to deepen people's understanding and appreciation of the cultural, artistic, historic, and natural resources of California and the American West. It operates under a 501(c)(3) nonprofit educational organization (Heyday Institute) and, in addition to publishing books, sponsors a wide range of programs, outreach, and events.

To help support Heyday or to learn more about us, visit our website at www.heydaybooks.com, or write to us at P.O. Box 9145, Berkeley, CA 94709.

Library of Congress Cataloging-in-Publication Data

Guilbault, Rose Castillo, 1952-
  Farmworker's daughter : growing up Mexican in America / Rose Castillo Guilbault.
    p. cm.
  ISBN 1-59714-006-6 (alk. paper)
  1. Guilbault, Rose Castillo, 1952--Childhood and youth. 2. Mexicans--California--Biography. 3. Immigrants--California--Biography. 4. Children of agricultural laborers--California--Biography. 5. Mexican American agricultural laborers--California--Biography. 6. California--Biography. I. Title.
  E184.M5G84 2005
  305.48'8680794'092--dc22

Interior Design/Typesetting: Lorraine Rath
Printing and Binding: Sheridan Books, Ann Arbor, MI

Orders, inquiries, and correspondence should be addressed to:
      Heyday Books
      P.O. Box 9145, Berkeley, CA 94709
      (510) 549-3564, Fax (510) 549-1889
      www.heydaybooks.com

Printed in the United States of America

10 9 8 7 6 5 4 3 2 1

To my parents, María Luisa Corral Rábago de García and
José Celedonío García Inclan, who inspired my dreams

And to my husband Richard, who made my
dreams come true

CONTENTS

Photographs follow page 96

1

VICAM, SONORA

The memories appear in dreams, like fragments of a broken kaleidoscope; deja vu triggered by a scent, a taste, a song. These blurry images evoke a time and place that was warm and comforting and protected me in a soft embrace.

I see the desert, vast and expansive, merge with the horizon. Saguaros stand still and idle, sentries silently guarding their domain of sand and heat where nothing moves faster than the measured slither of a snake.

Sonora. It's the desert exhaling hot, arid air. Air that's so still it stagnates and hovers like an invisible cloud. It's the omnipresent sun, a giant orange ball that drips heat onto the land, flat as the bottom of a skillet. To remember Sonora is to feel that heat. I know the desert temperatures drop in the winter and that it rains enough to flood, but these are not the images I keep stored in my memory cells. It's the heat that's scorched into my brain. Constant and unrelenting, yet reassuring in its consistency. Sonora, where I lived the first years of my life.

WE LIVED IN NOGALES, MEXICO, a hilly town bordering Nogales, Arizona. But my imagination only recalls Vicam, the small Indian village where my mother and I stayed for long periods of time with Aunt Julia and Uncle Nacho. My mother and her siblings grew up in Vicam. We were there often, and not just to visit while my salesman father traveled: my mother had her own business selling American clothes to townspeople who did not have passports to cross the border to shop.

By age four, I was a seasoned train traveler. The moment we arrived at the Nogales train station for a trip to Vicam, I became giddy with excitement. The mournful trill of the train whistle, groaning wheels grinding faster and faster, and the gush of steam underneath the tracks quickened my pulse with anticipation for the journey. The train, like a black desert centipede, inched its way through fields of sand, scrubby brush, and lonely saguaros. Towns flashed by—Imuris, Magdalena, Santa Ana, Hermosillo, Huatabampo—until the train ground to a halt in front of a platform shaded with a palm-frond roof from which hung a weather-beaten sign with faded letters spelling V-I-C-A-M.

In the 1950s Vicam resembled a page out of *National Geographic* magazine. The town was one of the eight villages in Sonora decreed to the Yaqui Indians in the 1930s by then-President Lázaro Cárdenas. They all have interesting names: Pótam, Bacum, Cocorit, Torim, Huirivis, Belem, and Rahum. My cousins and I had an ongoing contest—who could name all eight in the shortest time.

The towns were governed by a tribunal council that ruled on all matters including who was invited to be a resident. Long ago, for instance, it had been decided that all homes would not resemble those of the *Castellanos*. Homes built on Yaqui territory had to be made out of natural materials like adobe, wood, bamboo, and mesquite, in native architecture. The Yaqui elders did not want any discussion; these towns were for them, not the *Castellanos* who had caused them so much suffering.

Only a handful of "white" families lived in Vicam, mostly merchants who made their living selling merchandise to the Indians.

Uncle Nacho was half Yaqui. He owned a *tiendita*, a shrimp boat in Guaymas and, the most impressive, an outdoor movie house.

Nacho and Julia lived in a house that looked like all the others in town; a small adobe with a thatched roof, the ceiling inside formed with wood *vigas* and mesquite *latillas*. The floor was hard-packed dirt, swept and sprinkled with water daily to keep it clean and dust free. Indoor lighting was kerosene lamps, and cooking was done on a black iron wood-burning stove that took forever to light every morning.

My aunt's prize possession was a brand-new bedroom set given to her by Uncle Nacho as an anniversary gift. The queen bed with matching nightstands and bureau sat incongruously in the middle of the front room. It was the biggest room of the four-room house, serving as a living room, dining room, and bedroom. You'd walk through the front door and there was the bedroom furniture facing you, and then a small wooden table to the left and two wooden chairs on the right. My aunt, who always seemed to be sick, would lie majestically on the bed, chatting with visitors. Everyone acted as if holding court from a bed in the living room were perfectly normal.

Little had changed in Vicam between the time my mother was a young woman growing up and my own early childhood. Certainly more cars rumbled through the bumpy dirt roads, and the sound of better quality radios could be heard from inside houses, but no one owned a television set, nor did they have indoor plumbing.

Housework was completed by mid-morning, before the heat inhibited all movement. Afternoons were devoted to siestas and quiet activities like sewing. But the town came alive at dusk, when the air turned light and the soft suede nights were illuminated by the brightness of the stars and the moon. Chairs appeared in front of the houses, and neighbors promenaded through the streets, stopping to chat for a few minutes or accepting a seat for a longer visit.

Sometimes my cousin Georgina and I were allowed to attend Uncle Nacho's movie house. It was an open-air structure made of four high adobe walls and filled with long, flat benches in neat rows. It was built right next door to the house. The projectionist was elevated on a wobbly scaffold, and a long electrical cord extended a block down to the telegraph office, the only source of electricity in town.

Movies had long runs in Uncle Nacho's theater. The townspeople went two or three times to see the same film. Georgina and I were only allowed to go accompanied by mothers or older cousins, who of course never wanted us along. My mother didn't like to sit in the "theater." She complained that many of the Indians who attended were disgusting—belching, farting, and oozing body odor. My aunt claimed that lice jumped out from their hair. Uncle Nacho said they exaggerated. But the other "white" ladies shared their views. Consequently Uncle Nacho's patrons were mostly Indians. My mother and her sisters dubbed Uncle Nacho's movie house Teatro Yaqui.

But it was the Yaqui Indian culture that permeated the community. And it was not just the town's indigenous physical appearance; it was more intangible. There was a current of energy both magical and mystical in the molecules of the very air we breathed.

Their traditions, a mixture of indigenous beliefs and Catholic ritual, were both fascinating and frightening to a little girl. Converted to Catholicism in another century by Spanish missionaries, the Yaquis reverentially celebrated the major Christian holidays with a few pagan touches. The biggest celebration was Lent, culminating in Easter. There were the *Chapayekas*, metaphors for evil spirits and temptation, who appeared during Easter week dressed in phantasmagoric handmade costumes and masks. They marched through the streets playing tricks on people standing by, sometimes "stealing" children they would later return to unamused families. They terrified us children.

On Holy Saturday, *los Matachines* appeared in the church procession, dancing to the beat of a gourd rattle and holding a wand decorated with feathers in the other hand. At the fiestas the *Pascola*, dressed in a cotton blanket wrapped around his hips, bells dangling from a leather belt, and cocoon rattles encircling his legs, danced along with the Deer Dancer. The Deer Dancer wore a headdress with real antlers and a skinned deer face. Rows of seashells sewn onto leather leggings created the rhythm as he pranced around, imitating a deer.

We were told to stay away from these strange ceremonies, but a mixture of fear and curiosity constantly pulled me. My cousin

Georgina was a willing companion in these escapades. The Yaquis were not tolerant of white children hanging around, especially during their ceremonies. We were often chased away if caught or, worse yet, taken back to our mothers for the crime of "sneaking into other people's business."

"*¡Metiches!* You're going to get *piojos* from playing with Yaquis," my aunt scolded us.

Piojos (lice) were not the only thing to fear in the desert. We worried about scorpions falling on us from the ceiling where they crawled at night. The close howling of coyotes and wolves in the evenings when we slept outdoors in the back patio was alarming. And then there were the ghosts.

The same force that motivated us to chase Indians and spy on them compelled us to beg for nightly ghost stories. My mother and her sisters were master storytellers. Stories inevitably started with "This is a true story. It happened during the revolution to your grandmother."

Without television and radio to entertain us, our mothers' chilling tales (told by a flickering lamplight that cast shadows across the room) of family ghosts that haunted rooms where the *Cristeros* had buried gold or revolutionaries had hidden money captivated our imaginations more than any Stephen King movie would ever do.

They would pay the price later when whimpering, terrified children interrupted their sleep, swearing that spirits walked through doors, but I think my mother and her sisters, who enjoyed mischief and practical jokes, liked telling these stories as much as we liked hearing them.

— — —

I HAVE A RECURRING DREAM. In it I am a child, small and pale in a pastel-colored dress, walking alone on a dusty street. The sun glowers above me. Its brightness dapples the streets and buildings with light and shadow. People pass me but I cannot see them. They are like x-rays, dark, transparent, and faceless. I walk past

5

rebozo-draped women, a *Matachine* shakes his gourd rattle at me, lizards scamper across my path. Suddenly I'm running, aimlessly, frantically, through a tunnel where there was a street. An adobe house appears and I run through the door into its cool darkness. Inside a woman holds out her arms to encircle me. She smells of corn *masa*. Her body is like a soft pillow; it molds around me in her lap. Her voice is humming, bubbling like water skipping over smooth stones in a creek, her song a long sip of cold mountain water that quenches the dust in my throat, the thirst in my heart. I am falling deeply into the down of her body, contented, peaceful.

I awake startled, as if shaken by a firm hand, heart palpitating, sweaty and tired. I lie still, waiting for my heartbeat to slow down, reluctant to leave the place I've been. Because only in dreams can I recapture the sensory experience of my childhood in Sonora—where there were no seasons but that of the sun.

2

TITO AND MARÍA LUISA

TITO WAS A TALL, LEAN, GRACEFUL MAN. He wore his black hair neatly trimmed and parted on one side. He favored gray pin-striped suits and insisted his white shirts be crisp and stiff. He stored long, thin American cigarettes in a silver-toned cigarette case kept in his breast pocket along with a linen handkerchief. His cologne smelled like rainwater in a lemon grove, citrusy and fragrant.

All this I know about my father from my mother. I have few memories of him and little recollection of what he actually looked like.

You wouldn't call him handsome, my mother said. His nose was slightly crooked, his mouth too large, and his eyes too small for his long face. But his style, even his arrogance, made him attractive. His eyes, dark and limpid, were penetrating and intelligent, the exact shade of green found in Mexican river water. But they could also be hard and cruel.

He was born in Spain—his father Basque, his mother French. They lived in New York for awhile, but he grew up in Mexico City. My mother claimed his family owned a circus, later amended that to "a business," and finally admitted she really didn't know much about them. She never met them, he never talked about them.

"They're dead. That's all you need to know," Tito had said.

There were many things my mother didn't know about my father. That was the conflict from the very beginning, the reason my grandmother urged her not to marry him.

"You don't know his people. You only know what he tells you."

My grandmother's suspicions were rooted in the belief you only married a man whose family you knew. That way you could see where qualities and flaws began and predict the outcome based on the lives of elderly family members. My grandmother had practiced what she preached and married her first cousin.

In those days, my mother would later point out, there was good reason for small-town mothers to fear their daughters' involvement with unattached, out-of-town men. The quiet, sameness, and familiarity of their Mexican village life had been disrupted in the late forties by groups of young engineers, employed by the state government to work on a major waterworks project.

"We knew of at least two local girls who married these out-of-towners. They turned out to have families. Bigamists! What a scandal it was!" my mother recounted.

Tito was not deterred by his future mother-in-law's coolness. He courted my mother for many, many years, writing letters from throughout his sales territories in Mexico. When he came for extended visits he brought gifts—boxed vanity sets (the kind with a comb, brush, and mirror) or large plastic boxes of dusting powder.

María Luisa's family was not impressed. They dismissed *el Gachupín* as haughty and supercilious.

"He'd barely acknowledge us when he came to visit your mother," an older cousin recalled years later. "He'd stand at the front doorway and ask for your mother, never entering the house, as if it was not good enough for him."

My mother saw it differently. The tiny adobe house belonged to her married sister and brother-in-law. Along with their two children, they shared it with my mother, her mother, and three other unmarried sisters. There was no room for gentlemen callers, no privacy. My parents would take walks or ride in his car to have their conversations.

"We always had so much to talk about," she once told me.

"What did you talk about, Mamá?"

"Always the future. He wanted to do so many things. To be his own boss, run his own business. And I was to be his partner. We'd do it together."

"They were like movie characters to me," said a cousin who was a young boy at the time of their courtship. "I remember they liked to sing together. They'd stand right outside the front door singing, and family members would come from different parts of the house to hear them harmonize."

"Your father sang songs with double entendres, you know." My mother still smiled at the memory years later. "The one I recall the best is *'Quizá.'* He liked to sing it because I made him wait so many years before I agreed to marry him."

Siempre que te pregunto	Whenever I ask you
que cuándo, cómo y dónde,	where and when,
tú siempre me respondes	you always respond
quizá, quizá, quizá.	perhaps, perhaps, perhaps.
Estás perdiendo el tiempo	You are wasting time
pensando, pensando,	thinking, thinking,
por lo que tú más quieras	for what you want most
hasta cuándo, hasta cuándo	until then, until then.

My cousin remembers another song:

Humo en los ojos	Smoke in your eyes
cuando te fuiste,	when you left me,
cuando dijiste	when you told me
que ya te vas.	that it was good-bye.

"It seemed they were always arguing," my cousin would say. "They'd break up, then make up the next day."

Tito and María Luisa dated for ten years before they married.

"Oh, I flirted with others," she told me. An American geologist named Bill from a mining company, an engineer, and a professor. Before Tito there was one man I really wanted to marry but he was divorced and my mother absolutely forbade it. So there I was *una solterona* in my early thirties. I had to marry Tito."

"Did you love him very much, Mamá?"

My mother always stiffened when I asked this question. It's not that she wanted to avoid the issue, but that she wanted to answer truthfully, and the truth was complicated. I could see by her creased brow and thoughtful gaze that she was giving the question considerable weight. To say either she did love him or didn't love him, both would be half-truths. She treated romantic love like an abstract philosophy that could only be explained by rudimentary theories.

"Well, everyone believes in romance, but we often marry for other reasons. And there are different kinds of love."

TITO AND MARÍA LUISA MARRIED in a civil ceremony in 1951. My grandmother was too weak to attend but strong enough to say, "You've made your bed, now you must lie in it."

The newlyweds embarked on a whirlwind honeymoon, crisscrossing Mexico for a couple of months, with Tito conducting business along the way. My mother enjoyed the travel immensely but almost immediately became pregnant. It was too soon. He had wanted to travel more, just the two of them. After all, he'd waited so many years. But my mother was adamant: it was time to build a home life. Children needed a home.

"But I'm a traveling salesman. I'll hardly be home," Tito protested.

Nevertheless, they rented a three-room house in Nogales, Sonora, which bordered the American town of Nogales, Arizona. The location suited both of their needs as it was convenient to his business—selling products tourists would purchase in curio shops—and it was a three-hour train ride to my mother's family.

In late January my mother received a letter from my grandmother. "I dreamed you had a beautiful baby girl," it read. "She had curly black hair and pale white skin. You are so lucky to have a girl. She will take care of you, *mi'jita*."

I was born in February and my grandmother died in May.

3

NOGALES

IT WAS JUST THE TWO OF US, or so it seemed to me. My father was away so much he was nothing more than a tall shadow in the doorway, an impatient voice in the dark. His arrival was marked by two-toned shoes casually strewn in the front room, issues of *Selecciones* (the Spanish version of *Reader's Digest*) on the couch, and the ashtray once again filled with the long, thin cigarettes he smoked. His departures were marked by bulging suitcases by the door.

His presence disrupted the carefree days with my mother, running errands, shopping at the market, church on Sundays, visiting neighbors, listening to the radio, and playing *comadres* while she washed clothes in the tin tub in the backyard.

My aunt Hermelinda, known as Melinda, and cousin Lorena only visited while my father was away.

"There's not enough room for everyone if your father is here," my mother explained to me.

It was true. When Melinda and Lorena were around, their energy took over the house. They flew through the door like colorful birds, filling our drab space with a cacophony of laughter, chatter, and singing. Everything about them was overblown—if a dress called for one crinoline they wore three, and if a hairstyle required a braid they added two. Our days revolved around their activities—shopping trips across the border and flirtations with American border agents. Everyone said Lorena looked exactly like Sophia Loren and Melinda a Kewpie doll because she was petite with tight curly hair, a tiny waist, and twinkling eyes. A day or two before Tito was scheduled to return home, they'd quickly pack up the stylish, bright clothes, high heels, and bags of lotions, sprays, and creams. "Sorry we can't stay to visit with Tito. Oh well, until next time. Good-bye." And off they'd flutter.

—— —— ——

"YOU WERE SO HAPPY when he walked in from a business trip. You ran to hug him," my mother insisted years later.

I only remember his impatience. How he'd push me away after a hug.

"He liked to have his head massaged. He said it relieved his stress. And he'd always ask you to do it, said your tiny hands felt the best. You were so pleased he chose you."

Try as I might I could never remember that image. In its place was another one that haunted my sleep.

It started with the flash of flames rising from a burner. I'm turning the stove knob, curious, then surprised by the fire. My father is rushing in, startling my revelry with the dancing flames. A slap stings across my face. He's shouting as he grabs my arm, and then suddenly I'm thrown into a dark pit. Alone and cold, I hear my mother's voice on the other side, calmly reasoning. Cockroaches scuttle across the floor but I can't see them in the pitch dark and the sounds terrify me. "Mamá! Mamá!" I scream.

My parents' voices rise; his an angry thunder, hers a thin, reedy wail. A door slams and I am in the softness of my mother's arms.

I guess it was important to my mother that I recall the good parts of my early childhood. She put a happy face on every remembrance. After all, this man was my father and entitled to my automatic warmth and respect. That's how it was in her family. Family men had faults—her father had gambled, others drank, some went out on their wives—but they provided for their families, and that usually outweighed all offenses. The Catholic Church wanted families to stay together and considered divorce a bigger sin than carousing. My mother was a devout Catholic.

Or it could have been more complicated than that. She had lost her own father at eleven years of age, and her childhood memories had mingled with my grandmother's stories that glorified her young and all-too-human husband. The image of a lost, wonderful father who had loved her armed my mother with strength for many of her later trials.

When I think of my father, I think of his brown leather suitcases. He laid these plump satchels on their sides, opening them to reveal a treasure trove of merchandise. Out tumbled porcelain dolls, silver jewelry, regional Mexican dresses, onyx figurines of animals, and carved wooden boxes.

My eyes glittered with greed and longing for these colorful prizes, laid out so attractively. I'd hover around him until I'd sense his tension.

"Make sure she doesn't touch my things," he'd instruct my mother if he left the room.

My mother would wink conspiratorially, pick some plaything, and hand it to me. When he returned to the room she'd quickly take it back.

"You do have some nice products, Tito. You should do well," she'd say, replacing the object in the suitcase.

I'd stifle a giggle and my father would look quizzical, wondering what the joke was.

My mother occasionally talked him into giving me a trinket. He once reluctantly offered a small onyx elephant and another time he gave me a tiny silver knife and spoon.

But what I really longed for was a beautiful Mexican doll wearing the traditional *china poblana* costume, the dress associated with the Mexican hat dance. Oh, she was exquisite! Shiny black braids intertwined with green ribbons, and a black dress that glittered with gold and silver sequins outlining an eagle and a snake, like the one on the Mexican flag. She wore a white gathered blouse embroidered with tiny stitches and a red and green fringed rebozo curled around her shoulders.

The next time my father returned I waited for the magic suitcase to open. As he bent over to arrange his wares, my eyes scanned its contents, searching for my prize. I opened my mouth to ask him for the doll, but my throat closed. I couldn't find my voice. My mother walked into the room and I ran to her blurting, "Mamá, the doll is so pretty. Can't I have her?"

My mother smiled and stroked my hair. "Tito, can she have the little doll? She doesn't have one, you know."

"You'll spoil her by giving in to anything she wants," he snapped.

"You can replace the sample on your next trip."

He continued packing his case in silence. I clung to my mother's skirts, peering at the suitcase. It felt like hours before he answered. By the time he beckoned to me, I had figured the doll was not mine to have. My mother disengaged my hands from her skirt and, with a lift of her eyebrows, encouraged me toward him.

"Since your mother says you have no doll, I will give you your first one."

I stood very still in front of him, my heart pounding so fast and furious against my chest I thought for sure he was able to hear it. He opened his hand and placed into mine a small baby doll dressed in a tiny diaper and bonnet.

Tears of disappointment sprang from my eyes. It was small and ugly.

"So what's this? This doll isn't good enough for you? See what a little ingrate you're raising, María Luisa?"

"Take the doll your father gave you, *hija*. Just take the doll." My mother's voice sounded tight.

I never played with the doll. I left it outside the house until the paint chipped off, the tiny clothes disintegrated, and the white bisque chipped off to reveal brown extremities that soon wore into nubs. My mother found the pathetic doll discarded and abandoned behind the metal tub she used to hand-wash our clothes. She carried the naked baby, arms and legs now amputated, back into the house and carefully placed it in her cosmetics travel case.

"It's from your father. I'll keep it safe for you."

It was the last gift my father gave me.

4

A DOOR OPENS

IT STARTED WITH WHISPERS. Then muffled comments behind her back. Eventually the gossip had wound its way through the neighborhood grapevine.

People were talking about my mother and father.

It was my mother's good friend and neighbor María who sat her down.

"There's talk you should know about, María Luisa. It has to do with a woman who also lives in town, not far from here."

My mother paled but sat alert.

"People say she's Tito's mistress," María continued. "She has a little boy who could be your daughter's brother. I've seen them with my own eyes."

My mother did not take María's word even though she was a trusted friend. She searched for a woman with a little boy who looked like me until she saw him with her own eyes.

But that wasn't the cruelest blow. Someone else, somehow, somewhere, had passed on an even more disturbing story. These "friends" pulled my mother aside to inform her "for her own good," of course, that they had heard Tito had been previously married and, even though he was divorced, he maintained close relations with his ex-wife and children. Did she know this?

My mother was stunned. The news of a mistress was certainly unpleasant but this was devastating. Hiding a former marriage and family was a deeply wounding deception. It was like looking into Tito's satchel and finding it empty of the expected curios but overflowing with incriminating letters and films.

What else had he lied about? Had he ever told the truth?

My mother walked around the house like a sleepwalker, glassy-eyed and dazed. I watched with curiosity and concern. Mamá was acting differently. But not toward me. Even though she seemed unaware of her surroundings, her light touch and gentle voice reassured me that the cause of her gloom had nothing to do with me.

At night when we'd sit listening to the radio I watched her carefully, her face pale and drawn, staring blankly into space. Her eyes clouded and misted but no tears fell. She looked so sad. If I stayed up as long as possible, I could distract her, make her focus those vacant eyes on me, make her smile. But once I crawled into bed to listen to the radio playing the plaintive music of Agustín Lara or Javier Solís, my body relaxed and, too quickly, I'd fall asleep. On the radio a sweet-voiced singer strummed a guitar, interrupted by the occasional crackle of static. The flickering bare bulb on the shadeless lamp cast an enormous shadow around my mother, surrounding her with a phantom-like glow. Through my drooping lids I'd see my last image of the night: my mother reaching for the box of cigarettes, lighting the end of one with a long kitchen match. A haze of smoke enveloped her as she crushed one cigarette and lit another. The silence of her chain-smoking was interrupted only by the scratch of match against matchbox.

— — —

WAS I THERE WHEN HE CASUALLY WALKED THROUGH THE DOOR? I'm certain she told me the story only a couple of times, but it was described with such detail and clarity and still-palpable emotion that I've convinced myself I was an eyewitness.

She had considered all her options and was determined. She was prepared to give him an ultimatum when he walked in.

"You're a stupid woman," was his response. "Why would you want a divorce just for this?"

He hotly denied the mistress and argued he hadn't told her about his marriage and divorce because he knew she would have used it as an excuse to not marry him.

"We waited so long, María Luisa."

"Were you married during all those years we courted?"

He closed his eyes, emitted an exasperated sigh.

"Don't throw away our relationship because of something that has nothing to do with you and me. It was in the past, my past. It doesn't intrude on our lives now."

"You lied to me. How can I possibly ever trust you?"

The fight raged for days. He pleaded, cajoled, reasoned, and finally grew angry and defensive. In a voice as cold and cutting as a machete he said, "All right. You can have your divorce. You're a silly, hysterical woman. I misjudged. I thought you were smart and could be my helpmate and help me succeed in my business. I thought that's what we both wanted. *Qué lástima.*"

María Luisa simmered furiously but did not respond. Her eyes glowered at this man, her husband, suddenly a stranger. What did she really know about him?

"I'll want to take my daughter." He took careful aim to be certain his weapon made a deep and painful cut into her most vulnerable spot.

"Your daughter? What would you do with her? You can't even stand being around her for very long!"

"It doesn't matter. She belongs to me."

"No! You'll never take her! She's just a little girl; she needs her mother."

"We'll see." Tito turned on his heel and walked out the door.

— — —

"YOU CAN'T BE SERIOUS, MARÍA LUISA. There's never been a divorce in our family!" The Corral sisters were horrified.

"Let's be honest: Men play around, but Tito wouldn't leave you." Julia, who had married at seventeen, knew this from personal experience.

"*La gente decente* think divorcées are the same as prostitutes," sniffed Teresa, the social climber.

"Our mother will turn over in her grave! She never did like that man you married!" said Hermelinda, the youngest.

"Shut up, all of you! I can't believe you'd rather have me stay in a rotten marriage filled with lies and deception, just so others won't talk? I don't give a damn about *gente chismosa*."

But she did. She worried that she would be ostracized by the families whose children she wanted me to play with. She worried she'd never be able to remarry. That men would see her as tainted, damaged goods, already used by another. She worried she'd be excommunicated from the church, where divorce was not allowed. Most of all she worried Tito would carry out his threat and take me away from her. She knew that by confronting him about his transgressions she had hurt his ego. She had punished him with the ultimate blow. And now he was like a wounded animal, and he wanted to hurt her.

My generation would create no-fault divorce, but in my mother's time and place a woman was expected to endure whatever her marriage brought. It was considered shocking and unacceptable for a woman to seek a divorce, and what with the church, society, and family stalwartly against it, it took either enormous courage or folly for the woman to follow her moral convictions. These institutions would judge her harshly and always remind her it was she who chose her fall from grace.

It was in a muddled state of mind, distracted and upset, that my mother bumped straight into a woman while we were at the marketplace one day. Looking up to apologize, she surprised me by exclaiming, "Rafaela!" The woman turned out to be a distant cousin, one she knew more about from reputation than personal contact. Rafaela was considered a bit of a loose woman in the family. She lived in the United States and traveled back and forth alone. Her own children had grown up and she lived by herself. She was divorced.

My mother hadn't seen Rafaela in years, but soon they were chattering as if it had only been days. My mother invited Rafaela home and, over the course of the evening, poured out her troubles. I noticed it had been a long time since I'd seen my mother so talkative.

"What utter nonsense," Rafaela harrumphed, shaking the henna-colored curls on her head. She wagged a long, lacquered red nail at my mother, saying, "You have every right not to put up with *un hombre sinvergüenza*. Why the hell should you? Because of your sisters? They're not the ones married to him— and they're not the ones divorcing him either!"

She groaned impatiently, jumped out of her seat, and strode nervously across the room.

"Now, see? This is exactly what makes me crazy about Mexico. Yes, it's my country; I was born here. But these rules about women are so stupid. That's why I'll never come back."

Rafaela grabbed a cigarette, lit it, and inhaled in one fell swoop. I watched for the smoke to come out, but instead a steam of words shot from her mouth.

"You know I'm divorced. The jerk left me! But in the United States, what do you think?" She stood squarely in front of my mother, hand on one slim hip, eyes dancing with anticipated glee. "*En los Estados Unidos* nobody cares. The son of a bitch— that's English for *hijo de su madre*—is gone. I support myself. I own my house, I own my own business. I'm independent."

Rafaela, who had been thumping her chest with her fingers to make her points, now paused, searching my mother's face for her reaction. My mother seemed transfixed, her mouth slightly agape. I looked from one face to another. I'd never been allowed in such an adult conversation.

"And you know what I get from *los americanos*?" Rafaela stopped dramatically and lowered her voice as she breathed out one word: "Respect."

My mother sat mesmerized, unable to unlock her eyes from Rafaela's confident view of another world.

"María Luisa, you come to California with me. Get out of this cesspool. It'll pull you down and drown you. You're still young.

Start a new life in a new country. Both for you, and for your daughter's future."

Rafaela sat down on the coffee table facing my mother and took her hands into her own. My mother bit her lip and tears spilled down her face. Rafaela shook their hands up and down encouragingly. María Luisa responded with a tremulous smile.

5

LEAVING THE DESERT

WE LEFT THE DESERT AT DAWN. Pink rays of light streaked the steel gray horizon. The air felt cool and still. By mid-morning, heat would drip from the sun, a molten ball in the sky. But at 6 a.m. when we crossed the border from Nogales, Sonora, into Nogales, Arizona, the air smelled sweet and warm like the breath of a waking baby.

My mother's friend drove us across the border to the Nogales Greyhound bus depot. He left us standing near a handful of other early-bird travelers. We stood apart. My mother silhouetted against the dung-colored building looked glamorous in her freshly permed hair, stylish polka-dot short-sleeved dress, and black pumps. I wore a cotton pastel dress, white socks, and white Mary Janes. Our finery was new, purchased in the American department store La Vie de Paris in Nogales, Arizona. I loved shopping there. It was clean and cool. I never tired of hearing the piped-in music playing "The Poor People of Paris," which was played over and over. So much so that customers made up silly lyrics, *"Pobre gente de Paris, les cortaron la nariz."* (Poor people of Paris, they cut off their noses.)

My mother pushed me forward, urging me into the dark, cave-like interior of the bus. I climbed the steep steps and stumbled down the wide aisle. She impatiently scooted me into our seats. I yawned and rubbed my eyes. They felt as grainy as the sandy air of a desert morning. I snuggled into what felt like the plushest seat I'd ever sat upon—nothing like the train seats we rode on our frequent visits to see Tía Julia and her family in Vicam.

My mother sat ramrod straight, alert and tense. Outside my window the sky had lost its pink blush and the horizon shimmered with undulating waves of heat. I turned to my mother. She did not notice me, so intense was her stare at the driver who stood casually talking to a passenger in the aisle. I knew he was speaking English, a language neither she nor I spoke or understood. She had not noticed that morning had broken through the dawn. I wanted her to say something about it, as she did about every weather change. The Yaqui Indian servants of her childhood had taught her how to observe nature.

"*Ay, mira, hija,*" she would say. "The moon has a cloud around it. That means rain."

Or, "See the horizon? It's red and glaring. That means tomorrow will be another hot day."

I waited for her to speak, to tell me about the day's weather, about how it would be in California. But when her nervous eyes finally focused on me it was to scold gently. "You should go to sleep now. We have a long way to go."

The driver sat behind the large wheel and the long bus lurched forward. Soon we were rolling down a smooth road. I shivered from the air conditioner's chilly draft. My mother crossed herself and silently prayed.

After the prayer she sighed deeply. I must have looked concerned because she offered a small, quick smile and put her arm around my shoulder, rubbing me with her hand. Her warmth relaxed my body.

I was too sleepy to watch the moving landscape through the window. The motion made my eyes close involuntarily and I let my head sink into my mother's chest. I inhaled her familiar scent. It was reassuring and secure. She smelled like the desert.

Had I been older I might have shared her anxiety. I might have questioned the wisdom of a newly divorced, uneducated woman with a five-year-old child leaving her family and country in search of a better life. To be such a willing immigrant a person must have great optimism and little to lose. But my mother was leaving behind a great many things. Her family roots ran deep, to the sixteenth century when her Spanish ancestors settled in Batacosa, at the foot of the Sierra Madre. Siblings, aunts, uncles, cousins remained. No other family members lived in the United States, nor did they aspire to. Only our hostess, Rafaela, lived there and she was too distant on the family tree (having married a second or third cousin) to count as real family. It was on the thin thread of her invitation and encouragement to start a new life with her in California that my mother staked our future.

As a teenager I once asked my mother why she had left since she always talked about the greatness of Mexico. Maybe she had given up too much to come here, I suggested. She thoughtfully considered what I knew to be an impudent comment, and I immediately felt guilty. She shook her head sadly and looked into space, as if her gaze could travel back in time and pinpoint the precise moment she had made that momentous decision. Her eyes filled with tears—a given whenever she spoke of her life in Mexico or of her deceased mother.

"There was nothing to lose. There was nothing for you and me."

The day we crossed the border into a new country, a new world, my mother was not filled with optimism or the courage that comes from certainty. What I saw in my mother's rigid body and intense eyes was pure fear. Was she reexamining her decision? Whatever her concerns, they kept her tight-lipped and mute, squelching her usual talkative and extroverted personality. I would see this transformation at other times in my life—once on a road trip when the fog was so thick we could not see the road for miles ahead, and another time driving through the curvy, narrow roads of the Rumorosa mountain pass outside Tijuana during a snowstorm.

It was late afternoon when the bus approached the Salinas Valley through country roads. Miles and miles of green hills and valleys surrounded fields planted with a patchwork quilt of crops. White-faced brown cows dotted the hills. We passed towns so small the name was lost in the blink of an eye. Then there were no more towns, only vast fields watered by whirling sprinklers. In the afternoon sun, the water's mist cast hundreds of rainbows. I pressed my nose against the bus window and saw tractors driven by dusty men, dogs running alongside farm trucks, and an occasional child standing by a lonely mailbox, waving energetically as we passed.

"*Ya llegamos, Mami?*" (Are we there yet, Mommy?)

My mother peered over my head, outside the window. "Yes, I think we're almost there."

"It's nice. California looks nice."

My mother nodded and smiled. There was a glimmer in her eyes.

6

KING CITY

WE EMERGED FROM THE BUS at the King City depot in late afternoon. The depot was inside a hotel called the El Camino Real, and I guess the "depot" part was the small café attached to it. Then again, it might have been just the bench outside with the Greyhound sign hanging directly overhead. In any case, Rafaela was not there to meet us. We wandered inside the café to wait and order coffee for my mother and Coca-Cola for me. A couple of leather-faced men sat smoking filterless cigarettes and drinking inky coffee. They wore jeans and scuffed boots, and stained cowboy hats laid next to their seats.

"American cowboys!" I thought excitedly. Now there really was no doubt we were in the United States!

But even American cowboys couldn't hold my attention long that day. Everything seemed so different—the dark paneled walls, the curious smells, and the inviting room just beyond the doorway. I asked my mother if I could look through the door that led to the hotel sitting area. She seemed tense and nodded absently. Walking in was like stepping into the frame of a Western movie: worn brown leather couches and chairs were strewn throughout a large bright room, and murals depicting rodeo scenes graced entire walls. There were huge, ferocious bucking bulls and bow-legged cowboys dressed in leather chaps and tall hats, lassos swirling over their heads, with snorting, rearing horses. Another area featured smoldering iron brands poised in the hands of skinny cowboys aiming toward the backsides of complacent-looking cows.

"There you are!" Rafaela's high-pitched voice broke through my revelry. The tap-tap of her high heels echoed through the empty room as she walked briskly toward us. I noticed her figure-hugging flowered dress and new hairstyle. Red locks were piled high up on her head and not hanging loosely like last time we saw her. My mother followed her, laughing, her face relaxed.

"I'm late because I have so much to do at work! My God, I can barely handle so much work! My waitress quit today!" Her hands fluttered in front of her and I noticed her nails were still long and very red.

"Don't worry, Rafaela. I'll be happy to help out while I'm here," my mother soothed her.

"Oh, what a godsend you are, María Luisa! But you've come to change your life and I'm going to help you. You'll see." She winked at my mother and they both giggled. I didn't think what she had said was funny. I figured it was one of those grown-up inside jokes they never wanted to explain if you asked.

Driving to Rafaela's house, King City revealed itself like a penny arcade film. Pastel-hued houses with green lawns and borders of color-coordinated flowers flew by, replaced in the next frame by wide streets lined with mulberry trees and sprawling sycamores, followed by a sidewalk scene of blond-headed children balancing ice-cream cones on two-wheeled bicycles. I rolled down my car window and was rewarded with the sweet fragrance of newly cut grass. It smelled fresh and clean, so different from the dusty aroma of the desert. I gulped air, trying to absorb its essence into my pores before the scent faded in the breeze.

Rafaela's house was a white clapboard bungalow surrounded by pretty flowers she called "daisies." I decided these daisies were the prettiest flowers with the nicest name I'd ever known. Inside, the house was very small, just a bedroom, bathroom, and kitchenette. From the window, we could see a bigger house with a large yard surrounding it. Rafaela's daughter lived there with her husband.

The house belonged to Rafaela too, but she said her daughter was going to start a family and needed more space than she did.

"It's just more to clean. Besides, I spend so much time at work. I just come here to sleep some nights."

"Don't worry, Rafaela, we won't be in your way. We'll help you out," my mother assured her.

The next day, we started a pattern that remained during our stay with Rafaela. We'd leave early in the morning to her restaurant/bar, where we'd spend all day. Lunch was pretty slow, most of the customers came for drinks, some for dinner. Early on Rafaela would take advantage of the afternoon doldrums to take us calling on her relatives in town. There were Mike and Estela, Mila and Manuel, and Luz and Leopoldo. They were all from the Sonora and all interrelated. They seemed very old to me and very dull. Mike and Estela already had grandchildren. Mila and Manuel would have if they'd had children of their own. Only Luz and Leo were still raising a family, four daughters and one son. Their youngest daughter was only four years older than I. Theirs was the liveliest house, the one I liked visiting the best even though the older girls intimidated me.

My mother was pleased to find *gente decente* so far away in this small town in the middle of California's Salinas Valley. She noted that they all owned their homes. Owning a home was my mother's greatest dream.

"There's much to like about King City," she sighed one night as we lay together in Rafaela's guest bed, drifting off to sleep.

— — —

RAFAELA WAS PROUD OF HER RESTAURANT. It was the only place in town that served Mexican food.

In reality the place was no more than a hole in the wall, more bar than restaurant. A screen divided the bar stools from the handful of tables covered with brightly flowered oilcloth. It drew a steady stream of customers: Mexican farmworkers nostalgic for home cooking and American ranchers who liked drinking the beer more than eating the food.

My mother called the American customers "los caboys." They were coarse, blunt-talking farmers, ranchers, or ranch hands. And they liked flirting with her.

Rafaela noticed. Her gimlet eyes never missed anything. "That's what you need to do, María Luisa," she said decisively one night as they smoked their last cigarette before bedtime. "You must marry an American. It's your best chance for a good life here."

My mother looked down. "But I can't even understand what they're saying to me."

"You'll learn English. Look, all the Mexican men here are braceros. There's no future for someone like you with one."

My mother tried to take Rafaela's advice. We had quickly learned that Rafaela expected everyone to do as she told them. The cook didn't and left soon after another waitress.

My mother's increased time in the restaurant provided more time for her conversations with the customers, who were definitely interested in her. But it was Rafaela's final word that gave approval as to who my mother would go on a date with and who she had to turn down.

"He's got a nice car and house. No, he's lazy and drinks too much. Well, he's divorced but so what, so are you."

My mother had no problem being asked out on dates. The complication was that she always brought me along. That was the way it was done in Mexico. We soon found out why it was not done in the United States.

Mr. Brown had a nice, new four-door sedan and seemed to indulge her requirement that I come on their first date. I sat in the back and stared at his half-dollar-sized bald spot. That's about all I remember of the first time. Soon more dates followed.

"Do you like Mr. Brown?" she asked me

"I guess so," I shrugged.

Her face fell.

"He's nice. He brings me candy bars sometimes," I quickly added. I didn't want to hurt my mother's feelings if she really liked Mr. Brown, and I wasn't certain what I thought about him. Sometimes I felt he was nice to me just to please my mother. But who could be sure about anything? Between his broken Spanish and my mother's barely existent English, nobody understood anybody anyway.

It was not long before things became clear. It started like any other date. Mr. Brown came in his cream-colored sedan to pick up my mother at Rafaela's house. When she opened the door Mr. Brown grinned and pinned a corsage to her dress. She blushed with pleasure. I stepped out behind the door, grinning and ready to go with my coat over my arm.

His small eyes narrowed at me but he turned to my mother and half-whispered in his halting Spanish, "We're going to be a little late tonight. After dinner I thought we'd go for a ride. It'll be tiring for the little girl."

"It's okay, she'll be fine with us," my mother smiled reassuringly.

"I'm sure Rafaela can take care of her tonight, María," Mr. Brown persisted.

But my mother had already started out the door with me in tow. Mr. Brown didn't realize that my mother never left me in anybody's care. We had never been separated since I was born.

Mr. Brown took a deep breath and briskly walked toward us.

It was a fine night. We had a lovely dinner and afterward Mr. Brown insisted on going for that little ride in the country. My mother looked uncomfortable.

"I think it's late..." she started to say.

"No, no, María. I told you it was part of our evening. That's why I suggested *la niña* stay home tonight."

My mother forced a tight smile.

We drove onto a country lane. The road was very dark; only the car lights could be seen. In the front seat Mr. Brown reached over and pulled my mother to him. She demurred. Then he tried to kiss her, as if I couldn't see just because it was dark and I was in the back seat. She pushed him away, which caused the car to swerve. I sensed her fear and reached up and turned on the overhead light.

"Turn that off," scolded Mr. Brown. But I didn't know how.

He swung around, feeling the buttons until he turned the light off.

Once again in the darkness he tried to grab my mother. This time she cried an audible "No!" and once again I jumped up and turned on the light.

Mr. Brown's face was red, contorted with anger.

"You brat," he breathed between clenched teeth, swatting the air around me. I shrank away, digging my back into the seat as far as I could, more amazed than scared.

Suddenly my mother's voice demanded loudly and clearly, "Go home now. Home now, Bill."

Mr. Brown was remorseful the next day and came by the restaurant to patch things up with my mother. She would have none of him.

"He would punish her by hitting her," I heard her say to Rafaela. "I could never give her that kind of father."

7

New Beginnings

I MET JOSÉ FIRST. He was a semi-regular at the restaurant. Whenever he came in he always made a point of saying a few words to me. Silly stuff. Like "Hi, Howdy Doody." I didn't know what that meant but the way he said it made me giggle.

One day he asked me what cartoons I liked to watch. I told him we didn't have a television set.

"Well, you'll have to start saving money to buy one," he asserted.

"I can't work. I'm a child," I protested.

"Here, I'll help you get started." With that he took the can of Kerns peach juice I had just finished drinking, asked the waitress to rinse it out, and put a shiny quarter through the drinking slot. I ran gleefully to show my mother.

"The little girl needs tips for her savings account," José called out to the handful of men scattered around the room. "Go ahead," he said to me, pointing with his chin. "Collect your tips."

I glanced at the customers shyly, looking from José to my mother. My mother, who was sitting behind the counter drying glasses, seemed amused and nodded her consent. Nickels and dimes clanked noisily into the juice can, making a pleasant rattling noise when I shook it up and down.

From that night on, the tip can became a regular fixture at the restaurant—and so did José.

"I see you talking to *ese hombre*," Rafaela said one night.

"Oh, he's just a nice person. He misses Mexico. He hasn't been back for awhile and likes to talk about home," my mother answered airily.

Rafaela was sitting in a dressing gown mending clothes. She put her needle down and peered at my mother above her horn-rimmed glasses. My mother's face remained placid and Rafaela kept quiet.

It was clear that José and my mother enjoyed talking to each other. He'd make a few opening teasing remarks to me and then try to seek out my mother. But even when she joined in, talking as she removed plates and dishes, sometimes sitting for a few minutes with him, sometimes standing, he always included me in the conversation. I liked that. It made the evening in the restaurant go by faster.

We didn't go out with Rafaela anymore. She had lost yet another waitress and said she couldn't find anybody suitable. Instead, my mother worked every day, including weekends. The funny thing was that the restaurant wasn't all that busy. My mother stood around a lot waiting for the occasional customer.

José offered a break from this monotonous routine by inviting us to visit Mission San Miguel. My mother had told him about her desire to see all the California missions after being taken to Mission San Antonio, which was just outside King City.

"That's nothing," José told her. "Wait till you see San Luis Obispo. Now, there's a beauty. Then you've got to see Mission Carmel; it has beautiful gardens. And San Miguel and San Juan Bautista are also nearby."

My mother's eyes sparkled with interest.

"Invite some friends to come with us too," he added generously.

My mother asked Rafaela of course. She responded through tight lips, "I have a business to run."

Luz and her daughters were happy to come along. Luz said her husband Leo didn't like to go anywhere and it would be a treat to get out of her "rat hole." A friendship among all of us grew from those mission visits. My mother and I and even José were often invited for coffee and dessert at Luz's cheerful house.

"José is such a nice man, María Luisa," Luz said. "He's so good with your child, too. It's so rare."

None of this sat well with Rafaela.

"Why do you encourage that bracero?" she'd ask distastefully.

"He's a thoughtful man. He's kind to my daughter and generous with my friends," my mother replied patiently.

"Well, you'd better hurry up and help at the restaurant. We have a lot of work today." Rafaela scurried about, looking for her things.

"Rafaela, I'm tired today. It seems like I've been working six days a week for quite a long time. Besides, it's not all that busy."

"What are you saying? That I'm forcing you to work? *You* offered to help me out."

"Yes, of course I did. But it's not like I'm a paid employee..."

"Oh, so that's what this is all about? I help you, but your help comes with a price tag? Is this how I get paid back for extending a helping hand to a relative?" Rafaela was so upset her chin began to quiver.

My mother shook her head, mortified. "Rafaela, you misunderstand. I'm very grateful for all you've done for us. I wouldn't dream of taking money from you. Let's put this behind us. Come on, let's just go to work."

Rafaela's eyes still flickered flashes of ire, but she clamped her jaw shut and appeared to accept my mother's resolution.

But the tension did not go away. Rafaela's manner cooled. She took to announcing in front of my mother "Your bracero is here," loud enough so José might hear. If my mother complained, Rafaela claimed it was "just a joke." At her house Rafaela hardly spoke to us, feigning fatigue. There were no more cigarette chats with my mother before bedtime. I watched Rafaela go through her nightly ritual as she wordlessly prepared for bed. I was like a nervous rabbit around Rafaela, on alert in case her mood or temperament changed suddenly. She brushed her hair, spread cold cream on her face, and rubbed it pink with tissues. She greased her elbows and heels with baby oil. Then, with a perfunctory "good night," she turned off the lights.

I saw my mother chewing her lip throughout the day. It worried me but I didn't know what to say to her or what to do.

I wanted to go up to Rafaela and demand, "Why are you being mean to my mother? She hasn't done anything to you!" But earlier I'd heard her barking at the help. Her whole personality had changed. It was as if she was someone I didn't even know.

One afternoon my mother overheard her tell someone on the phone that María Luisa was a *malagradecida*, an ingrate.

My mother confided in Luz. What could she do to straighten out this terrible misunderstanding? Luz, who had known and observed Rafaela for many years, shrugged and said, "Rafaela has a difficult personality. Sooner or later she turns on everyone. That's why she can't keep a husband or hired help."

José went further: "She wants to control you—to work for her without complaining, see who she wants you to, and think what she wants you to. You don't need to suffer this. You've suffered so much already. I can't bear to see you treated like this. I want to take care of you and live to make you happy."

— ◆ —

"Do you like him mi'ja?" she asked me gently.

"Yes, he's very nice, Mamá. Do you like him too?"

She smiled and nodded. I didn't realize I had just given her my blessing to marry him.

The profundity and weightiness of the decision she placed so lightly on me like a shawl would not be realized for years to come.

Rafaela accepted the news with a sardonic grin and a shrug. "You've already made one mistake, you know. You said you wanted so much for Rosela, but now all she'll be is some farmworker's daughter."

My mother's jaw tightened. Her eyes reflected both anger and hurt, but she said nothing. Instead, she raised her head and left the room with me at her heels.

José and María Luisa married in Mexico with my Aunt Teresa's approval. She gave my mother a stylish black crepe wool dress with a satin bow in the back for her wedding and held a family reception afterward in her house. The newlyweds left me

with Aunt Teresa and her six children while they went on a short
honeymoon. I felt proud when my female cousins raved about
my new father, insisting he looked exactly like the American
singer Frankie Lane, whoever that was. I can't remember making
the mental transition of realizing that the nice man in the restaurant was now my father. I just know it was a natural flow. It was
as if José had always been Papá and Tito was no more than a
recurrent dream.

8

WE MOVED INTO AN APARTMENT ON PEARL STREET. It was part of a large, rambling white clapboard house belonging to Mrs. Maggie and Pete, whose family had once filled all five bedrooms. Rather than letting them sit unoccupied gathering dust, they'd converted some into apartments and the house, of curious architecture to begin with, had been remodeled to accommodate this new enterprise. The units were located on the main street, and around the corner on a side street was the house's main entrance, adorned with a picket fence and primrose pathway. To reach our place you had to walk up ten long wooden steps that ended in a landing facing four doors. Three of those doors led to apartments, the largest of which was ours. It consisted of a small bedroom, front room, and tiny kitchen. There was no bathroom. That was the fourth door. We had to walk out our front door and unlock the bathroom door to use it. Nevertheless, we had the private bath our landlords had promised since we were their only tenants at that time. I don't recall the bathroom being a problem, although I'm certain my mother complained about its inconvenience.

The property had a large backyard—big enough for a grape arbor, a vegetable garden, and a dilapidated garage that housed an old tin lizzie. It was a delightful playground, as long as Mrs. Maggie didn't spy me picking strawberries or pinching grapes from her perch inside the covered porch that overlooked the yard. She disapproved of all the activities I found particularly fun.

The best part of living in Mrs. Maggie's boardinghouse was the location: it was close to every place that mattered to us—the grammar school I would attend, the post office, Tri's Supermarket and, of extreme importance, Mr. Papandapoulos's grocery store. He stocked the most extensive variety of penny candy in town, possibly in the world. Practically a whole aisle of boxes and boxes of anything you could possibly crave: hard fruit-flavored candies, chocolate kisses, Bazooka bubble gum, gumdrops, licorice, too much else to mention.

Across the street from us lived my mother's new acquaintance, an old lady named Mrs. Bane. I liked to visit her house with my mother because it was filled with treasures. "Junk," my father called it, but it held wonders for the very young and old. The house had three oversized windows that hinted at its previous function as a Mexican restaurant. Oriental rugs covered her living room floor, hiding the yellow linoleum. A horsehair couch draped with a fringed Spanish shawl sat in the middle of the room with a zebra rug spread out in front of it. Next to that was a huge lion-skin rug, its shaggy-maned head lay with its mouth gaping in a permanent roar, teeth bared, eyes glazed in final terror. The eyes looked so real I had to touch them. I was surprised when they moved in their sockets.

"Oh no, *niña*. You don't touch my lion," Mrs. Bane scolded. She spoke Spanish and claimed Spanish heritage. Her skin was brown and smooth like mahogany, and her black hair streaked with silver was pulled into a neat bun held together with Spanish combs. Mrs. Maggie said she was a Jolon Indian and had been a woman of "reputation" in her day. When my mother asked why, Mrs. Maggie pursed her lips and spat out, "She was an entertainer. Went up and down the valley performing for men."

"Why, I sang for Randolph Hearst himself," Mrs. Bane bragged to my mother. "I'd play the guitar and sing Spanish songs and dance."

It was hard for me to imagine Mrs. Bane, who looked like a Beatrix Potter character in her full dresses covered with oversized aprons, singing and dancing for anybody.

"Sing one, Mrs. Bane," my mother pleaded cheerfully.

The diminutive Mrs. Bane in her long skirts and tiny shoes needed little encouragement. She ambled to her upright piano, banged the keys energetically, and warbled a vaguely familiar tune.

"Ah, you of course recognized *'Cielito Lindo'*? Sung just for you, my Mexican friends."

I looked with amazement at my mother, whose eyes twinkled with mirth.

"That didn't sound like *'Cielito Lindo'* at all, Mamá," I whispered.

"Mrs. Bane was probably a very good singer in her days," my mother insisted.

There were many things in the house Mrs. Bane didn't mind if I played with. Like her basket filled with ostrich feathers, her boxes of sepia postcards, and the stacks of black-and-white magazines that featured people wearing old-fashioned clothes. While my mother and she chatted, I'd leaf through the yellowed sheet music on her piano and try to decipher the names of songs on her 78 records. When I got bored doing that, I'd ask to go to the bathroom, even though I didn't have to go, just to snoop on Mrs. Bane's frilly vanity table. It was dressed in cabbage-rose chintz and held a fascinating array of fragrant bottles and creams. Her bed was decorated like a young girl's—all ruffles, lace, and embroidered pillows. Even the room smelled romantic, of verbena and violets. At five years of age, I found all these curiosities very entertaining. Much better than visiting Estela, her friend who lived down the block and only had *Popular Mechanics* magazines in her living room.

My mother, however, wanted me to play with children my own age and not just visit her *viejitas*. But the American children who lived across the street were standoffish. When I tried to approach them, they acted funny because I couldn't speak English and had no patience for sign language games. When I tried to communicate, the crew-cut-haired neighbor boy and his pedal-pusher-wearing sister would stare at me, scrunch their faces, and say, "Wot? Wot?" At least that's the way it sounded to me.

So my social world consisted of my mother's old lady friends and a furry cat my stepfather brought me that my mother christened "Missy Fu."

Our landlady, Mrs. Maggie, was a plump, impeccably coifed, silver-haired woman who maintained a standing weekly beauty shop appointment and always welcomed the opportunity to socialize. She spoke enough Spanish to get on and would often invite us to watch her old-fashioned big brown box TV with the small screen. We were thrilled to be included. In Mexico we'd only had a radio and listened to *novelas,* music from the *época del oro,* and my favorite, the *Cri Cri Children's Hour.*

Mrs. Maggie would knock on our door in the evening to invite us for some TV viewing. My stepfather would quickly clean up, my mother would smooth her hair, and we'd rush out the kitchen door, which opened onto a screened porch. Gingerly we'd walk around the steep cellar steps that led to Mrs. Maggie's canned preserves, wind our way through the narrow kitchen single file, and make the few steps down the hall and into the parlor. Chairs placed theater-style waited in front of the TV.

These invitations first trickled in as weekend treats, and then as we became more and more integrated into the couple's daily life, our visits were a nightly routine.

But it was never a totally comfortable arrangement. The heavily curtained parlor was cold and dark and smelled of old wood. Framed prints of somber-looking Indians and deer-head trophies looked down on us. Dark wood wainscoting covered the walls, giving the room an austere, foreboding feeling. In this eclectic setting we were introduced to shows like *Lawrence Welk, Ed Sullivan, Gunsmoke,* and *I Love Lucy.* We all had our favorites. My father preferred Westerns, my mother Lawrence Welk (or Don Lorenzo Gwelk, as she called him), and I the *Mickey Mouse Club.*

Inevitably conflicts arose. Mrs. Maggie gabbed incessantly in English, Spanish, and a strange language that sounded suspiciously like a mixture of both, I couldn't tell for sure. She had a knack for breaking into commentary at inopportune times, such as during the Champagne Lady's solo or my parents' favorite polka. Her husband, Pete, seventy-odd years, was another story. He wore a hearing aid the size of a sliced cantaloupe and spoke so infrequently we were always surprised to hear his gruff voice. During Mrs. Maggie's rare lulls, he'd startle us by suddenly demanding in an unusually loud voice, "What'd he say?"

I had my own problems with Pete. Although Mrs. Maggie was sympathetic to my Mickey Mouse mania, she had to defer to Pete's baseball obsession.

Baseball season found Pete slumped in his cracked-leather easy chair, his good ear tuned into a tinny sounding radio all afternoon. He strictly forbade TV viewing or any other activity during game time. But I had noticed, by lurking around, that he regularly fell asleep during the games, and always well before the *Mickey Mouse Club* came on. Once Pete fell asleep, I could have clashed cymbals next to his ear and he wouldn't wake up. The trick was making sure he was sound asleep before sneaking in and turning on the set. If he wasn't, there'd be hell to pay!

After two whole days of sneaking in and sidling up noiselessly next to him only to have him resurrect with a sudden "What do ya want?" I had my chance. I knew it by the thundering snores shuddering from the chair. I tiptoed toward the TV, glancing only briefly at Pete's outstretched, inert body. My hand shook slightly as I turned the knob. A burst of glare flickered on the screen. Just when Tommy, Doreen, Jimmy, and Annette were making their appearance, a horrible sound came from Pete's direction. I spun around to see his arms and legs flailing about as he sputtered, "God dammit! God dammit!" (one of the first English expressions I learned, much to my parents' dismay.)

On my way out, I passed Mrs. Maggie in the kitchen. She must have figured out what had happened by the commotion and my long face.

"You know Pete loves his baseball," she said gently.

But I was obsessed. I ran down the street to Estela's house, overcoming the discomfort I felt at her dour and cool manner. I begged to please "borrow" her set to watch the *Mickey Mouse Club*. At first she obliged. But after a few times, she stopped answering the door when I came over, even though I could see her look out the corner of her window. I felt so hurt, I ran home and told my mother.

"Why, you little pest! You can't bother people for their TVs!" my mother said, shaking her head.

I wanted to cry, but instead I swallowed hard and waited for the urge to pass by playing with a scab on my knee.

"Well, we'll just have to get our own TV," she said soothingly.

Not long after that, my father showed up one night with a spindly-legged set that, even though brand new, always had a snowy picture.

More than anything, that first TV symbolized our connection to America, our window to a new culture. Language isolated us, but the simple storylines of the shows we watched gave us a better glimpse into being American than observing our next-door neighbors.

We especially loved the Westerns: *Gunsmoke; Have Gun, Will Travel; The Rifleman; Bonanza;* and, on Saturday afternoons, *Roy Rogers.* There were good guys and bad guys, horse chases, shootouts, and straightforward values. Just like in Superman comics, truth, justice, and the American way always won out. The Westerns were easily digested, entertaining, and comforting in their message: be honest, work hard, and you'll be respected and have a good life. Westerns were so uniquely American. They reenforced what we believed to be American culture.

There was one TV character we could relate to directly, and that was Desi Arnaz. The fact that we didn't know any night club performers, let alone anyone who played congo drums for a living, didn't interfere with our identifying with the immigrant husband of Lucille Ball. What we saw in our living room was a handsome, successful Latino making it in an American world.

Watching Desi Arnaz on TV was like having a distant relative nearby. He tossed out a few Spanish words in each episode, sometimes sang Spanish songs, and had an obvious accent. My parents referred to him as "el Desi," a term of familiarity. If others saw him as a silly Cuban with a funny accent we certainly did not and would have been shocked to know that perception even existed.

Desi Arnaz was our symbol of success, and by rooting for him we subconsciously cheered for ourselves to do well in this new land.

9

The Farm on Jolon Road

THE GLEAM IN PAPÁ'S EYES and his swagger as he stepped into the room tipped us off he had some exciting news to tell. But we couldn't ask outright; I had learned that his news was revealed in its own good time. Prodding from me only resulted in teasing and further prolonged the delivery of information. I knew my mother suspected Papá had something to say because she searched his face expectantly every time he started to say something. Finally, after dinner, he pushed his plate back, slurped his last bit of coffee, burped contentedly, and was ready to talk.

"Licha," he smiled at my mother. "The family that's been living in the smaller house on *el rancho* is moving away. Don Ray has offered us the house rent free."

Papa looked quite pleased with himself, but a shadow crossed my mother's face. "It's so far from town," she said carefully.

"Well, I know you like living in town. But we can't afford to buy a house right now. And I don't know how long it'll take to save up if we keep renting. I just thought we could save money a lot faster if we lived on the farm for awhile."

My mother's dream was to own her own home. The seeds of a deep-seated longing were planted when her mother had sold the family house after her husband's death. My mother was eleven years old when her father died suddenly, and since that time she had lived in a series of homes belonging to others. First, two rooms in the city where the next-door neighbor ladies emerged only at night. Then they were rescued by a former servant who took them into her already full home because she could not bear to see hard times befall her kind former employer's family. My grandmother declared that her pride did not permit her to go back to her unsympathetic in-laws begging for a hand-out. She preferred to accept this caring hand and work as a seamstress to support her family. The five sisters and mother crowded gratefully into the room spared for them. The one brother was given a cot in the backyard and a mat for the living room floor in the winter. When my mother's sister Julia married an older, more prosperous man at age seventeen, they all moved in with them at his invitation. But Julia, immature and flushed with the good fortune of owning her own home, lorded her position over her sisters, making arbitrary rules of what they could and could not do in "her house." When they protested to their own mother, my grandmother—weary of the sibling battles and her own life struggles—shrugged, "It's her house. She makes the rules."

The house in Nogales was just another transition; my mother longed for the real thing.

"When I have my own home, the kitchen will be the largest room in the house. We had a large kitchen when I was a child and some of our best times were spent there." Here she'd pause, allowing herself to give in to the revelry of the fantasy. Her eyes would soften and a smile would play on her lips, making her look like a child leafing through a Christmas catalog. "There'll be a large backyard so I can plant my flowers and herbs and of course vegetables too. And I'll also plant apple, apricot, and lemon trees, maybe even fig and almond trees. I want a house that's airy, with big rooms and lots of light."

My mother would collect and save things waiting for this perfect house. She'd crochet doilies for coffee tables and the backs of sofas and chairs, embroider pillowcases and table-cloths. She bought blue ceramic fish to hang in the blue and yel-low tiled bathroom she would have, in the meantime keeping them wrapped in tissue paper in the closet along with all the other pretty things that would one day decorate her home.

She found houses that might be suitable but they would elude her grasp. The timing was wrong, the money wasn't there, or my stepfather feared the encumbrance. And even when she finally owned a house, it was not the home of her dreams, and she kept searching, still dreaming of that perfect place.

One day I found the blue ceramic fish tucked away in the recesses of an overstuffed closet. One of the fins was broken but she just shrugged, no longer caring about the tiled bathroom or the pretty decorations that now smelled moldy from the dampness of years. Maybe she realized that the childhood house where she was so happy, and that she had tried so hard to replicate, was gone like the heap of crumbled adobe that was all that remained of her own home in that faraway village in northern Mexico.

So when Papá reasoned with her that living on the farm for a few years was a shortcut to buying a house, my mother agreed. But she was still skeptical. The move would take us away from conveniences, she argued—grocery shopping, the post office, and what about school for Rosela?

"We're not moving to the mountains," Papá laughed. "There's a school bus that picks up all the farm kids. We'll come to the post office and the grocery store on Saturdays."

"But I'll need to learn how to drive," she added.

"And I'll teach you. On the farm. There's lots of empty roads for you to practice without hurting yourself or others!"

Mamá laughed and it was settled.

THE FARM ON JOLON ROAD was miles out of town without a name or sign to identify it. If you missed the dirt road entrance that led to the farm, you could wind up at Mission San Antonio. In time, however, I would learn that the lack of signage did not render the farm anonymous. Locals identified farms by their landowners' names or the people who leased the farmland.

"I live on the Doud Ranch on Jolon Road," I could say and townspeople would nod in recognition.

In the late 1950s, when we moved to the farm, the Salinas Valley was a prosperous farming community producing a cornucopia of crops: juicy tomatoes, plump purple sugar beets, and leafy lettuce. It reigned as the "lettuce capital of the world" and the "salad bowl of the U.S." It was a kingdom of bounty where the farmer was king. The effect of a good crop could be seen in the spring when brand-new pastel-hued Cadillacs appeared on the streets like blossoms on a tree.

But on the day we moved into the white clapboard house on the farm, none of this was significant to me. I was filled with excitement because I would have my own room and Papá had promised I could have a puppy in addition to Missy Fu, our cat.

The farm looked welcoming on that golden day, the sun shining like amber and the fields strewn with yellow bricks of hay.

In front of our house was the boss's office, a small square wooden structure. A few yards away loomed a huge barn from which men emerged driving different kinds of trucks and tractors. Beyond the barn and next to the fields was a smaller barn-like building I later learned was used for storage. Down the hill was the bracero housing, where single men who worked in the fields lived in a series of barracks.

On one side of our house was the road and open fields, and if you walked straight across to the other side, through a grove of eucalyptus trees, you'd reach the boss's house. There was also a barn and a corral, a water tower, and yet another storage building on the property. And on all sides, surrounding all these buildings, were acres and acres of fields. They stretched all the way to the purple mountains that fenced them in, giving me a sense I could go no farther in the world than those foothills.

10

School Days

I HATED SCHOOL. I hated leaving home every day. Home was safe, warm, and constant, without the conflicts I had to endure in the outside world. But I couldn't tell my mother that. She was so full of optimism.

"Oh, you're going to learn so many things. American schools are the best in the world! You'll be so smart because you'll know two languages." Her face shone with enthusiasm when she said these things, and I didn't want to dampen her spirits.

Her words suppressed my childish complaints. But even if I had dared share my feelings with her, I didn't yet have the vocabulary to explain the bigger issues that were the real source of pain, nor would I understand them myself for years to come. At six years of age, I lived in a world of confusion—the language, the kids, the culture spun around me like a vortex. Within one year I had moved away from family and the stability of a routine to a foreign country with a foreign language. Then we moved from town and our newly established relationships with friends and neighbors to an isolated farm where I had to readjust again and, now, school.

Each day presented challenges and I had to sort through them by myself. Even if I wanted to ask for help, what exactly would I ask for? Help me understand what the teacher is saying, or stop the kids from treating me like an oddball?

I intuitively knew that the person I leaned on for everything—my mother—would not be able to help me. She relied heavily on her own experiences as a basis of understanding the world, and just as the Wizard of Oz had nothing in his bag for

Dorothy, she had nothing to smooth this assimilation for me. Once I stepped outside my door, I was all alone and had to fend for myself. The only thing I feared more than school was disappointing my mother, so I hid my anxieties.

Every morning, she walked me the full two miles to the school bus stop and stayed with me until the bus arrived. The boss's boys walked by themselves and stood on the opposite side of the road, not talking to us while we waited. It set the tone for a curious relationship. They weren't unfriendly, but neither were they forthcoming. Their whole family couldn't decide whether to treat us as subordinate employees or as neighbors.

I was glad to have my mother with me. Cattle roamed on one side of the road and the bulls liked to bellow and chase us along the fence. Their snorting and hoofing terrified me.

Leaving my mother and boarding the bus brought up still more fears. The big yellow bus was filled with high school kids who were to be dropped off first before we continued to the elementary school. The older kids laughed at me, and I couldn't understand most of what was being said. They'd often not let me sit next to them, stacking schoolbooks alongside empty seats when they saw me approach. I learned to automatically walk quickly to the back and sit by myself. I found all of this confusing and humiliating.

At school things were no better. The teacher's instructions would wash over me like a wave; I heard the sounds but didn't understand their purpose. But eventually, slowly and unexpectedly the English language revealed itself to me. Every new word and every new definition was like lifting a layer of film from my eyes, giving me clarity to see the world around me. Words empowered me and I pursued their secrets assiduously. At home all I had was an ancient English/Spanish dictionary my father had used to teach himself English, but its tiny print and archaic language did more to obscure meaning than shed light on it. I actually learned more from the grocery store–bought encyclopedias, which I read cover to cover one summer. By the end of first grade I was scholastically on track: I knew the alphabet, wrote in block print, and could read the "Dick and Jane" books. By second grade, my English was much improved. My interest in books also heightened with the acquisition of a library card, and it helped that the library was conveniently located across the street from San Lorenzo Elementary School. I loved the feel and smell of hardbound books at the library. I delighted in sitting quietly, trying to decipher the mysteries between their pages, mainly by interpreting the illustrations.

But for all my struggles in the classroom, my greatest challenges occurred on the playground. The girls talked about things I knew the words for but had no point of reference on. They talked about birthday parties with cake and games like pin the tail on the donkey and musical chairs, barbecues with hot dogs and root beer, and toys I'd never heard of.

One day Mona said we should bring our dolls to play with at recess. I wanted desperately to fit in, so I stuffed an old baby doll—the only doll I owned—into a paper bag.

"Why are you taking that paper bag to school?" my mother asked.

I knew she wouldn't understand why I'd want to take my doll, so I fibbed. "The teacher asked us to bring our dolls."

My mother raised an eyebrow but chose not to pursue the matter.

At recess, the other girls all pulled out their dolls. It made me want to laugh out loud—they'd all brought the very same one! I proudly pulled out my baby doll. Nobody had one like her!

"What is that?" Mona scrunched her nose at my doll. "Don't you have a Barbie?"

The other little girls twittered. What was a Barbie? I wondered. And why was my doll looked down on? I felt embarrassed and quickly stuffed my unworthy toy back into the paper bag. I would not be invited to play with them again. Nor would I be invited to Mona's or any of the other girls' birthday parties.

And that's why I hated school. Cultural gaffes were far more difficult to overcome than language gaps. I felt like an outsider, and I would not be able to shake that sense of alienation throughout my school years in King City.

My mother tried her best to be supportive. Surely she sensed my disaffection when I trudged home down the long road, looking weary from another day in the outside world.

"My teacher Mrs. Lewis doesn't like me," I confided once. "I'm always in trouble because she says I talk too much."

"Do you?" my mother asked gently.

"No. I just answer the girl next to me, but I get in trouble, not her."

The following week my mother insisted I take a tray of homemade enchiladas to Mrs. Lewis. I had to carry them on the school bus wrapped in a brown grocery bag. Even the high school kids couldn't hide their curiosity.

"What's in the bag?" they asked over and over.

I was mortified. What would they think if I told them I was taking food for my teacher? I'd seen some kids bring apples, but never an entree!

I refused to talk and huddled in the corner of the bus by myself, clutching my package.

"She's a retard," a high school boy said disgustedly. And that, mercifully, stopped the questions.

Once we reached the grammar school I nervously walked straight to my classroom, avoiding the playground. I arrived breathless. Anxious thoughts popped into my head. What if Mrs. Lewis was disgusted and threw the dish into the trash can. Or worse, acted superior and asked, "What is this? Does your family actually eat this?" I would not be able to bear it if Mrs. Lewis expressed any form of rejection toward my mother's offering. I would simply never go to school again!

"Why, what's this? It's not time to come in yet." Mrs. Lewis looked up from her desk when she heard me close the door.

"My mother sent you this." I thrust the package in front of me.

She put on the glasses that hung from a gold chain and often rested on her ample bosom, and strode toward me. Mrs. Lewis was plump but moved quickly.

She took the wrinkled package and unwrapped it carefully on her desk.

"Enchiladas!" she cried out. "I love enchiladas! How did your mother know?"

I shrugged happily. How *did* my mother know?

"Bless her heart," Mrs. Lewis clapped her hands together. "Homemade enchiladas!"

From that day I can honestly say I was treated differently. Mrs. Lewis was more patient and attentive after the gift.

But not all situations could be solved with homemade enchiladas. I wanted my mother to be a part of the classroom culture. I wanted her to be like the popular kids' mothers, to be a room mother so I would fit in with my classmates. But she couldn't because she didn't drive or speak English. Another teacher suggested she make cupcakes for classroom celebrations instead. I thought this presented a great opportunity to be accepted by the class. I had observed how kids whose mothers made cupcakes were given special stature by the others.

It didn't work out quite so easily, though.

"I don't know what a cupcake is," my mother said, perplexed.

"It's like a little cake. But it's in a wrapper," I tried to explain.

"I can make empanadas for your party. They're probably similar," she offered.

Now, I knew there was no similarity between empanadas and cupcakes other than their both being desserts, but my mother insisted I ask my teacher if she could bring them. I had a bad feeling about it, but I went ahead and asked anyway.

"Oh no, dear," Mrs. Steussy demurred. "The children only eat American things. Have her bring cupcakes."

Mama learned to make cupcakes by deciphering a recipe from her new Betty Crocker cookbook. The other mothers baked theirs in colored papers or pretty tinfoil cups and decorated them with candy and little umbrellas or flags or plastic figures identifying the occasion. If it was St. Patrick's Day, the cupcakes were green with little leprechauns on top. For St. Valentine's Day, white-frosted cupcakes would be decorated with red candy hearts and coordinated red foil cups.

But my mother's cupcakes never turned out like the other mothers'. Hers looked like pale muffins haphazardly spread with a glob of thin, runny white frosting (made from C&H confectioner's sugar and not Fluffy Frosting Mix). My classmates looked at the box lined with wax paper instead of colored tinfoil like the others and whispered "yuck." A knot formed in my throat and I silently swore I'd never ask my mother to make anything for class ever again. It was the beginning of a subconscious effort to keep my private life and school life separate. If the other kids didn't know about my home life, they would assume I was like them. I could be American at school just like everybody else. And as long as anyone who really mattered never came to my house—which was not difficult since we lived way out in the country—they'd never know the truth.

11

BOOK OF DREAMS

OUR FAVORITE PUBLICATION as new immigrants was the Sears catalog. This "wish book" was a metaphor for America's bounty and what could be had with hard work. It was a book that came to our home and from which we could leisurely, conveniently, choose anything we could possibly want and have it delivered to our doorstep. The concept was amazing to us. This wasn't about accumulating goods but about obtaining a piece of the American pie.

Many of today's immigrants are easily caught in this country's web of overconsumption, easy credit, and easy debt. But in the early sixties, the values in rural areas were different.

Every new catalog was savored. We all had our own favorite sections. Papá, eyes sparkling, would ease himself into his chair after dinner and examine the tools, hunting rifles, and cameras. Then he'd pass the catalog to Mamá, who—for what seemed to be hours—studied the pretty dresses, household appliances, dishes, and linens.

By the time the catalog made its way into my hands, my palms itched with desire. At Easter, I would lose myself in pages of frilly pastel dresses with matching hats and purses. In the Christmas season, which brought my favorite edition of the year—the thickest one—I would sit for hours staring glassy-eyed at the pages and pages of toys, dolls, and games.

But we never ordered anything frivolous. The inside of our farmhouse was sparsely furnished with hand-me-down furniture from the boss, except for the TV and a cheap, nylon forest green sofa set my father had bought my mother as a wedding gift.

Extravagances were unaffordable. Only the most practical and necessary items could be bought, like my mother's first washing machine, a school coat for me, and thick dark-denim overalls to keep Papá warm in the frostiest of dawns.

The Sears catalog also had other uses. I'd cut out the models and use them as paper dolls, and my mother would match English words with pictures: *"¿Estas ollas, serán 'pots' en ingles?"*

Many years later I acquired a 1941 Sears catalog. I enjoyed looking at the old clothing styles and reading and rereading the two stories it had on typical Sears customers. One profiled the Browns of Washington State, who arrived as homesteaders, lived in a tent with their children until their farm produced enough for them to build a two-room shack, and eventually built a comfortable farmhouse on their land. Photos showed Mr. and Mrs. Brown with their new cream separator, daughter Evelyn with her new Elgin bicycle, and the whole family listening to their Silvertone radio phonograph—all from Sears, of course.

The second story described the Yeamens of Glendale, in Los Angeles County. Mr. Yeamen worked at Lockheed Aviation, a mile and a half commute from the family's "modern, five-room bungalow...with a barbecue grill in the backyard and a view of the mountains from every window." Photographs showed the various family members with their Sears products: Dad relaxing on a glider swing in the backyard, Mom putting avocado sandwiches in lunch boxes, and the kids romping in their stylish clothes.

The Browns and Yeamens, the catalog summarized, are what all of us want to be—"good, solid, dependable Americans."

As corny and blatantly commercial as those stories were, I enjoyed reading them. I thought it modeled what Americans were really like. These were, after all, real people, not TV characters. Even though my family of Mexican immigrants probably didn't have a whole lot in common with the Browns and the Yeamens, we too shopped from that Sears catalog—a book that made us believe everything was reachable and ours to have, just as it was for every other family in America.

And just like the people in the catalog, my family prospered too. Not in great leaps and bounds like the Browns of Washington State, but little by little. Our progress was marked, of course, by the occasional splurge from the Sears catalog.

When I got to the point where I had to own my own clarinet or drop out of the elementary school band (there was a limit to how long we could borrow from the music department) my family had to make a choice. I was not a great musician, we all knew that, but the band was a wholesome activity that integrated me into school life—into America—and so it was important to me. One evening after dinner, my parents called me into the living room. I searched their faces for a clue, but they remained mysteriously impassive until my father revealed a wrinkled brown package hidden behind his back.

My heart began pounding when I saw the Sears return address. Then, out of the bag came a compact gray and white case, and inside, lying on an elegant bed of royal blue rayon velvet, were the ebony pieces of a brand new clarinet. Never in my stolen afternoons with the Sears catalog had I imagined possessing something so fine!

A newspaper article would later describe the Sears catalog as "the best record of American material culture." But to many of us, this catalog transcended materialism. It was about making dreams come true.

12

SALINAS VALLEY SEASONS

I SOON LEARNED THAT LIFE ON A FARM was dominated by the seasons, each with its own rhythm and personality.

As an only child, I would find myself often isolated and alone. But I was befriended by nature, who delighted and stimulated my imagination. I became a keen observer of the seasons, eagerly monitoring the landscape's changing palette.

In the spring the naked hills and land grew verdant coats of glossy grass, and sprouting seedlings poked their green heads through the moist earth. But it wasn't until after Easter, when the sun radiated sufficient warmth to coax open buds, that wildflowers erupted in color over the hills and through the meadows. Purple lupine, orange poppies, acres of yellow mustard, pink irises—all grouped together like an Impressionist canvas. If Easter was early that year the March winds would blow cold early in the afternoons, bending the grass blades so far back they undulated as I imagined they would on an English moor. Springtime excited all my senses. At dusk, the sweet smell of alfalfa and a hint of honeysuckle perfumed the cool evening air.

In the mornings, the freshness of newly sprouted grass invaded my nostrils, and my mouth watered, anticipating the "green" taste of a tender blade's moist sweetness. My ears acquired radar, and I detected subtle sounds: the *sft-sft* of gophers impatiently shoving dirt out of their winter nests, the *thump-thump* of baby rabbits against soft dirt (warning me I was too close), and the *zift-zift* of lizards racing behind bushes.

I'd sit still and silent, my back against the sun, waiting to see what might appear. My patience was rewarded. Between the blades of grass, beetles cleared paths, ants loaded with cargo quickstepped, and grasshoppers jumped so high they landed on my legs. Sometimes I saw animals emerge from winter refuges: garter snakes slithering through the brush, or baby hares leaping out of bushes like fluffy jacks-in-the-box. Even a reticent doe might appear, proudly walking a wobbly-legged fawn along a field. If I held my breath and sat perfectly still, they might come close enough for me to see the fawn's dapples and the twitch of her nose.

Early mornings when I awoke to go to school, dawn entered dressed in a transparent veil of fog. Dampness clung to the air as I walked to where the dirt road met the paved blacktop, where the yellow school bus picked me up.

If spring was sublime, summer was frenetic. The farms down Highway 101, up Jolon Road, and through Loanoke Road became a beehive of activity, abuzz with fieldworkers, tractors, and harvesters that picked, packed, and boxed a salad bowl of crops. Vegetable packing shed conveyor belts hummed into action. Centipede-long trucks lumbered up and down country roads, loaded with boxes of tomatoes, lettuce, carrots, or sugar beets spilling over the containers. Fieldworkers in colorful clothes dotted the green fields like flowers. The pungent smell of ripening fruit and vegetables overpowered everything else, and years later, with the production of garlic, the southern portion of the valley reeked with that odor.

Midsummer saw the hills shed their emerald coats for gold, and the only green spots that remained were the leaves of madrona and oak trees.

School was out and summer meant days so long that no matter how many activities I undertook, they would not stretch to fill the time until day's light faded, well past my regular winter bedtime.

Mornings started warm and sultry. Bees droned monotonous tunes outside my bedroom window, swarming the sweet-smelling flowers my mother had planted "so you will have sweet dreams."

I'd do my chores—make my bed, feed the chickens, sweep the porch—and have the rest of the day stretched before me like a lazy cat. I might contemplate riding my bike down to the Salinas River and pretend I was searching for treasure, but that was a forbidden pleasure. I couldn't take the chance that my mother's warnings about quicksand by the river were true, especially having seen all those Tarzan movies in which the bad guys die slow, watery deaths. Later I would realize it was her fear of the vagrants known to roam the riverbanks that led to this white lie.

On hot afternoons when there was nothing to do but give into the heat and be lazy, my mother and I entertained ourselves by telling stories. My mother's tales were a mix of family histories, legends, myths, and religious lessons. She'd also include story lines from movies, radio dramas she'd heard, and *novelas* by Corinne Tellado from her favorite magazine, *Vanidades*. My mother possessed a rich, mellifluous voice that insinuated itself into my imagination, tugging at my emotions and commanding interest through her uncanny knack for mimicry.

I'd sit back, mesmerized, in a trance, letting my imagination wander through her verbal imagery. My mind was the movie screen, her voice the projector. She encouraged me to share fresh new stories with her too, and I desperately wanted to read lots of books and be able to tell her enthralling tales like the ones she told me. My only disappointment on my trips to the library was that I could not check out more than three books at a time. Summer was my father's busiest work season and he could only manage to drive into town once a month.

When school resumed in September, the fields lay ravaged and the stench of squashed, rotting vegetables permeated the air. There was no doubt summer was over. The autumn winds whistled mournfully as they danced with whirlwinds of dust over the plant-littered earth. Soon the fields would be cleared, leaving the once-lush land bare except where yellow bales of hay were strewn like gold bricks.

In town the streets slowly emptied each week as migrant workers headed back to their homes. The town looked abandoned and felt lonely. No longer did teenage boys stand on their usual street corners in their best black pants, white T-shirts, and freshly pomaded hair, smoking and calling to each other. No longer did the tinny sound of the accordion playing *ranchero* music escape from the swinging doors of El Resbalón, the farmworkers' favorite saloon. Even the torrent of cars that flowed down Broadway became a trickle. Texas license plates disappeared, not to be seen again until spring, when once again the orange plates would sprout along with the California poppies to brighten the gray, empty streets.

My father's work consumed him. He left home before dawn and worked into the night, harvesting one crop and clearing for another. This season offered the greatest potential for overtime, and I learned the meaning of the expression "make hay while the sun shines." The uncertainty of winter loomed. If it rained, he would not work and therefore would not be paid. He had no contract, no benefits. So he drove the tractor from sunup to sundown, and prayed the winter would bring enough rain for steady work in the summer and fall, but not so much as to put him out of work in the winter and spring.

Winter arrived like a ghost, its presence felt before its physical appearance seen. Cold, damp, foggy mornings descended on the valley, covering the fields with sheets of crunchy frost. The linoleum on my bedroom floor was an iceberg. I raced to the bathroom every morning in my stocking feet. My teeth chattered like rattles and goose pimples swelled and scratched against my thin flannel nightgown. The wood stove in the kitchen provided the only warmth in the house.

Outside, the hills and slopes lay fallow, waiting to be plowed in neat rows and wavy patterns. The birds were gone, the animals hidden. Winter was a stark world of muted colors: dark brown hills and fields, deep blue skies, and foamy, thick, white morning fog.

Mamá made oatmeal every morning. As much as I disliked its mushy texture and lumpiness, nothing else could warm my insides and prepare me for the long walk to the school bus. Girls were not allowed to wear pants in my grammar school, and so morning after morning I'd stand waiting for the bus hunched over, shivering against the cold and wind as my legs grew stiff and blue from winter's chill. In the coldest of winters, when the wind blew frigid and unrelenting, not even my warmest coat could keep its icy fingers from making my spine shudder.

After school the bus deposited me at the same spot I'd started out, but the road back home always felt longer. The cold pummeled my back. It made my nose red and drippy and irritated my eyes. Only the aroma of my mother's cooking warmed me the instant I opened the door. Suddenly, the bad weather, demanding teachers, and clannish classmates—external struggles that could be as trying as seasonal changes—did not matter as much. In my house, our little nest, familiar food, favorite afternoon cartoon shows *(Quick Draw McGraw* or *Yogi Bear)*, and the lightness of my mother's cheery patter made the dark season bearable.

Then the rains came—in torrents, drenching the hard-caked soil and encircling the countryside with their gray cloak of desolation. Would this be the year the complacent Salinas River turned into a raging tide and flood? Would the crops be ruined or improved? Would there be enough work for Papá?

No animals. No flowers. No people. No answers. Just black, rich earth all around, redolent of musk and dampness.

The land lay ready, wanton for seeding, eager to procreate in the spring, when the cycle would start all over again. Another season. Another crop. Another year in the life of a farmworker's daughter in the Salinas Valley.

13

MIGRANT SOULS

I WAS NOT THE ONLY ONE who observed the seasonal rituals. For migrant workers, the Salinas Valley was just one stop on the work trail they followed. Their comings and goings with the seasons were integral to our lives.

There were two types of migrant workers: the Mexican men who worked the six-month agricultural high season (generally June through November) and the Mexican families, who came from Texas or border towns like Mexicali, children in tow, working their way through California's various harvests.

The men who arrived alone from Mexico led mostly ascetic lives. They worked Monday through Saturday and preferred it that way. Some found the energy to go into town Saturday nights, but most were seen in town only on Sundays—at church and later at restaurants and bars. To them the United States meant work and, therefore, their lives revolved around it. They woke with the chill of dawn and returned in the cool of dusk to their bare, crowded, cell-like rooms.

I'd see these men piling out of trucks and trudging up the long dusty trail at the edge of the field that led to their housing. "*Pobrecitos.* Poor men," my mother would say. They resembled battered birds—straw hats covering hair matted gray from layers of dust, and ragged, thin shirttails over mud-splattered khaki pants.

Were the men young or old? I don't recall, although they must have been young because their voices, carrying ahead of their steps, were always filled with laughter. Their inflection hinted at jokes being told.

I noticed they never joked when the boss was with them. During those times, they maintained a respectful silence, broken only by a wink or a smile directed at me as they passed by. Did they see the reflection of a daughter or sister in a skinny little girl?

Once inside their small whitewashed cabins, the sounds and smells of their nightly rituals permeated the air. Percolating coffee, the sizzle of frying food, the buzz of conversation. A lone voice wailing a *ranchero* song of lost love and longing segued into silence and soft darkness. Later, crickets continued the mournful song.

Maximiliano, or "Maxi," as everyone called him, was one of these men. He first came to California in the 1950s under the bracero program, which brought thousands of Mexicans to the farmlands of the United States. Maxi often stopped by our house at night to talk with my father, usually outside beyond the front porch, a respectful distance from the family.

"What do they talk about, Mamá?" I'd ask.

"Manly things, *hija,*" she'd answer.

But once a year, some time in the fall, he'd appear right there on our porch, freshly bathed, hair smoothed down with brilliantine, white shirt gleaming against his brown skin, to announce his departure for Mexico. Maxi was lucky—he had a green card—but like many of the men who went back and forth across the border legally, he never seriously considered bringing his family to live in this country. Why? Because they could enjoy the best of both worlds. My mother offered this insight: "They are the story of the grasshopper and the ant. But in their case, they're grasshoppers for six months and ants for the other six."

On that last day of the season, when Maxi would come to say good-bye, I'd see him silhouetted against the porch light, his front gold-rimmed teeth sparkling from his broad smile as he described the latest letter from home. The babies were walking, talking. He and his wife were well on their way to buying their own home. Next year he could start putting away money to purchase a gas station; he wouldn't have to do this backbreaking work for much longer. Five more years, he figured. That was the only reason he kept coming to the United States.

With Maxi's departure, winter seemed to descend immediately.

Around May, Maxi would return, new straw hat in hand, rested and plumper, ready for another season. Once again those migrant birds would pop up on the streets—first a couple of men, then a half dozen families. By June a bustling new population had infused the town with its spirit. The musical cadence of Spanish conversation echoed through the grocery store, post office, and streets. "It's beginning to look like Mexico around here," grumbled some of the townspeople.

They came from Texas—Douglas, Brownsville, Reynosa—or other places in California—Porterville, Calexico, or the San Joaquin Valley. The families would stay until school started and then leave by October or early November at the end of the carrot and bean season. The Mexicans from Texas, *los Tejanos,* as we called them, spoke loudly, using expressions my mother and I didn't recognize. Words would start in English and end in Spanish. I wouldn't learn about "Spanglish" until college, so back then I simply accepted what my mother said: "*Pobrecitos,* they have their English and Spanish all mixed up!"

Summer and fall were abundant times. They brought work, food, jobs, families, and friends not seen since the year before.

Luz was one, a special friend. She hailed from Brownsville, Texas, and was older than I. Unlike most of the Texas migrant families, she came only for the summer. She stayed with a married older sister in Brownsville during the school year so she wouldn't have to miss class like most of the other migrant kids, who were always pulled out to work with their families. Luz did well in school and she had already decided to become a nurse. She would never be a migrant gypsy like her parents, she vowed.

Somehow Luz had learned something I hadn't—that one had to assimilate in order to progress. Whereas she had made a point to associate with Anglo kids at school, I wasn't that calculating.

My friends were mainly Anglo because all the Mexican kids I liked never stayed long enough for us to develop a relationship.

Once I asked Luz what she told her friends back in Texas about her summers.

"Oh, I tell them I go on vacation to California. And you know what they say? 'Oh, Luz, look at you! You got such a nice tan. You must have spent all your time on the beach.'" Her mimicking voice carried a trace of bitterness.

Luz did become a nurse and Maxi continued his trips back and forth to Mexico until he retired at sixty-two. His family always remained in Mexico, where he was able to provide a higher level of education for some of his children. He eventually managed to buy his own home, but the gas station never panned out. "Somehow there was never enough money," he said.

14

UNCLE JANDO

THE DECEMBER I WAS EIGHT YEARS OLD, we travelled back to Sonora. In Vicam my mother rented a car and driver for twenty-five American dollars. She wanted to see her brother Alejandro, who still lived in Batacosa, the village where they were born. My Aunt Julia said Batacosa depressed her and she would keep company at home with my father, who also wasn't interested in the trip. My mother insisted I go with her.

There were no paved roads into Batacosa. Drivers had to use potholed pathways or follow the curve of the dry riverbed that led to the edge of town.

The day was sticky and overcast for December. The twenty-five-dollar car's gears squealed indignantly at each shift as it lurched painfully across the desiccated river bottom strewn with rocks. It jostled us so violently I slid across the back seat into the opposite door. I entertained myself by picking at the frayed rubber that dangled from the inside of the window, watching it disintegrate between my fingers. The opaque windows were stuck open one inch, allowing dust to fog the inside and insinuate itself into my nostrils and throat, triggering a cough attack.

"Here." My mother pushed a handkerchief over my nose. "Don't inhale the dust."

"I can't breathe, Mamá," I gasped.

She sat next to the driver in the front seat, straight and prim.

"Good heavens, señor. Is there no way to keep the dust out of this car? My child is choking!"

"If dust is all we have today, señora, we'll consider ourselves lucky," the heavyset driver said good-naturedly.

"We sure wouldn't want to be caught out here in a *chubasco*."

"No, of course not." Then my mother looked suddenly confused. "But it's not *chubasco* time."

The fat man reached to scratch his dusty head, revealing a yellow perspiration stain under his short-sleeved white shirt. "Weather's been funny this year. Everything is turned around. Never know what to expect," he shrugged.

Outside, dust blurred the road like a cloud of smoke. I strained to see beyond the shadowy mesquite trees, searching for signs of the village and Uncle Jando. My mother said Uncle Jando rode a sleek white horse, dressed in Western clothes, and insisted on wearing fine leather boots.

"The last time I saw him, he looked like a tall, skinny cowboy," she chuckled.

"Like one of the Cartwrights?" I asked, referring to characters on the show *Bonanza*.

"Um, no."

"Like Rowdy Yates?"

"Well, more like Mr. Favor, I guess. He kind of looks like Mr. Favor except his nose is different."

For someone who was a fan of the TV Western, the idea of having an uncle who resembled the trail boss on *Rawhide* provided great fodder for my fantasy world, a place I played in more than in reality. I imagined Uncle Jando tall and handsome astride a muscular palomino greeting us as we stepped out of the jittery car. He'd remove a tan cowboy hat and his horse would dance a little, like the horses in the Mexican *charreadas*.

"Care to ride my horse?" he'd ask me in a husky voice. I'd nod shyly. Grasping me with one strong arm he'd pull me onto the magnificent beast and off we'd trot. My mother would stand beaming as she waved a handkerchief calling, *"¡Cuidado, Alejandro!"*

"Here we are." The driver's voice startled me out of my reverie.

"Dios mío. Nothing has changed," my mother whispered. Her eyes reflected the faraway look of a sleepwalker. I followed her

gaze. A cluster of narrow adobe houses spread before us surrounding a dusty *zócalo*. In the center a white kiosk badly needing new paint stood empty. Four wooden benches were the only embellishment. The lack of trees and greenery gave the little *zócalo* a forlorn, neglected appearance. We drove silently through an arch and past a small weather-beaten sign announcing "Batacosa."

"Over there," she directed the driver to a house that looked like all the others.

"It was my grandfather's house," she told me. "I grew up playing there. My grandmother always had treats waiting for us, glasses of milk with squash and brown sugar. Or *empanaditas* filled with *panocha*." She let out a long sigh.

Chipped white plaster exposed brown adobe on the outside walls of the house. A high sidewalk (so houses wouldn't flood during frequent rainstorms) curved around the narrow front steps that led to the bright, recently painted blue front door.

We got out of the car and dusted off our new dresses. My mother snapped open her red pocketbook and brought out a lipstick tube and mirror. She hastily applied a pomegranate red color to her faded lips and plumped up her new perm. The driver walked toward the kiosk, patting a pack of cigarettes into his shirt pocket while my mother and I ascended the steep stairs.

Uncle Jando did not open the door. Instead we were greeted coolly by a stout woman in a black dress with hair pulled into a severe bun held with Spanish combs.

"Tía Lupe!" my mother threw her arms around the old woman. "It's your niece, María Luisa!"

Recognition flushed Tía Lupe's cheeks, cracking her cement-like face into a tight smile.

"Ah, *la americana* returns. Come back to see how the poor survive."

Tía Lupe stopped then, seeing me for the first time. "Is this your child? *A ver, niña.*" Tía Lupe's hard eyes swiftly appraised me. "She doesn't look like you at all, María Luisa." She made it sound like a compliment. "Come in. Let's have something cool to drink."

The corner of my mother's mouth twitched but she only murmured sounds of appreciation.

"Jando's had to go to the panhandle to herd some cattle that got loose. He'll be here shortly."

"It's been such a long time, Tía Lupe," my mother began. "I have so many memories of this old house, of being a child here."

"Yes, you and your sisters just have memories. You all left as fast as your legs could carry you out of here. Except Jando. He's the only one that appreciated his old aunt."

My mother's eyes flashed darkly. She pulled higher her already ramrod-straight back and briskly replied, "Surely you aren't blaming us for seeking better opportunities, Tía Lupe. How would we have survived in this *pueblo* without a father and a sick mother? We had to leave!"

María Luisa nervously smoothed her navy blue and red cotton dress. It was the latest style, a short-sleeved, wide-belted, full-skirted dress, like the kind Donna Reed wore.

An old Indian woman shuffled in then with a tray of lemonades. I gulped my glass down and waited to be asked if I wanted more. No one did, so I shyly poured some myself. It was oversweetened and burned my throat.

The Indian woman, her face brown and creased like a walnut, walked across the cement floor toward an old dark cabinet, returning with a glass dish of hard candies, multicolored and stuck to each other.

"Go ahead, take one," my mother urged, seeing me hesitate. "It's very gracious of Tía Lupe to offer you sweets."

My usually talkative mother seemed to be having a difficult time keeping the conversation going with Tía Lupe. Their talking started up and died down, like the engine of our rented car.

I concentrated on sucking a butter-flavored candy, enjoying the coolness of the adobe. The sitting room was sparsely furnished with only a horsehair sofa and two cracked-leather chairs with cowhide throws covering the backs. On the walls two old-fashioned oval portraits of a stern-looking couple watched over us. Above me wooden beams with crossed *vigas* held up the ceiling. The room felt like it was closing in on me, and I shook myself and started kicking the chair back and forth with my heels.

"Maybe you'd like to go outside on the patio and see my animals?" Tía Lupe said. My mother looked relieved.

From outside I heard their voices rise and fall excitedly. I turned my back with disinterest. I was glad to be out of the strange room and away from the even odder conversation taking place. My mother wasn't acting quite like herself, but then again, I had begun to notice how my mother's personality always seemed to change whenever she was around her family.

The house was built in a U shape. At the far end a fence closed off the U, and next to that was a corral with pigs and goats. Around the inside patio, chickens and turkeys scratched and pecked at the ground. I ran toward them flapping my arms, scattering them. I laughed at their scolding clucks.

The groan of a gate being opened diverted my attention from the animals. A tall, loose-limbed man with a pinched face walked through. His battered and stained straw cowboy hat overwhelmed his head, making him look like a scarecrow. He rubbed his skinny thighs as he limped, half dragging his pointy boots. He must have seen my shadow by the corral because he turned cautiously toward me like you do when you think someone's staring at you. He grinned and I noticed a couple of missing teeth. Then he scuttled away as if embarrassed.

"*¡Mi'ja!*" my mother's bell-like voice rang into the courtyard. "Come and greet your Uncle Jando!"

The sugar from the lemonade and candy felt like it had curdled in my stomach. *That* was Uncle Jando? He looked as much like Mr. Favor as I looked like Shirley Temple! I felt a stab of disappointment in my stomach. Why did she always have to exaggerate?

When I reentered the house, my mother and her brother were there alone, Tía Lupe having left to do something or other.

"Jando, this is my little girl." My mother pulled me next to her on the sofa.

The long, hollow face nodded amiably, its eyes soft and warm as a deer's.

"*Hermano*, it's been too long," my mother said, reaching for one of his callused hands.

"Well, I guess I saw our sister Julia about two years ago, and you I haven't seen in a long time."

María Luisa's eyes glistened and she bit her lip. "You're so far from all of us. Mamá was right. When you decided to live with Tía Lupe, she took your body and soul! She's the one that kept you from us. It doesn't have to be that way, Jando."

Jando fidgeted uncomfortably in his seat, massaging his thigh. "Ah, it's not her. It's the town. I've been here too long." He avoided my mother's open face, as if he'd already said too much.

"Hurt my leg last week. Horse threw me. Let's go to the other room. I need to lay it out."

She grabbed his arm solicitously, shaking her head at his injury. The gangly scarecrow of a man and the plump lady in the stylish clothes looked funny together, I thought. It was hard for me to imagine them as brother and sister.

In the next room, Jando sat on a highback chair and put his foot on a stool. A small faded blue table held a tin cup, newspapers, and cigarettes. He reached for the pack and offered a cigarette to my mother, who nodded and sat down. I glanced at the chipped walls. Pictures of mysterious Mexican saints hung above a sleeping cot along with a crucifix and a dried palm leaf shaped like a cross.

Jando and my mother smoked and made small talk while I looked through the wooden slats on the windows. Beyond the tiny *zócalo* I could see our driver sitting on a bench snoozing, and behind the tired adobe houses were the mountains, dark and mysterious.

"What I'm telling you, Jando, is that you can start a new life. You can be a bracero and make more money in one month than you make in one year eking out a living in this godforsaken place." My mother's tone was insistent.

Jando inclined his head toward her, listening intently while he twirled a filterless cigarette in his yellowed fingers.

"What's California like, *hermana*? And your Salinas Valley?"

"It's green like the cactus in spring, *hermano*. Rolling hills and valleys. Rich and fertile lands. Not like this barren land you're trying to coax weeds out of." She leaned toward him, warming to the subject.

"In the summer the fields are filled with every vegetable imaginable. Tomatoes, corn, lettuce, carrots—and they all grow healthy and big. There's orchards too—cherries, pears, plums. And there's work for everyone." The words rolled off my mother's tongue like a song.

"Hm," Jando sighed. He gave a little closed-mouth smile, perhaps self-conscious of his missing teeth.

"Would they really hire someone like me?"

"Of course, Jando. You're an experienced rancher and farmer. Why, most of those poor devils are ignorant *campesinos* from the mountains. They might even make you a foreman when they find out all the knowledge you have!"

"But I would also be a *campesino* there. *Un pobre diablo*. I'm my own boss here. It's my land."

"It's *her* land."

"But I'll inherit it."

Jando looked out the window. His gaze seemed to seek out the majestic mountain that stood like a canvas outside his door.

"I've lived here all my life. Never wanted to leave before..." His voice faltered.

"That's why I've come. I want you to come to California with me. I don't want you to suffer anymore slaving for this old woman. She took you from our mother when you were a little boy so she could make you her personal slave. That's what you've been all these years, Jando. A hired hand. Look at you! In your early thirties looking like an old man because she works you so hard. She'll never give you the land, Jando. She already took it from us after our father died. She won't give it back!"

Jando stood up abruptly, knocking over the stool. "You shouldn't say those things."

"They're true, Jando. You know they're true."

He waved his hand dismissively and walked to the door. Silence permeated the room like a fog.

"It smells like a *chubasco* is coming." He sniffed the afternoon breeze authoritatively. "If you stay much longer, you might get stuck here because of the rains. Roads will be too muddy."

"Jando, I want you to come with me. Today. Pack a bag and come to California with me."

There was a clatter of hurried footsteps on the wooden sidewalk outside. "*Señora, señora.* The people are saying a *chubasco* is coming. We have to go," the driver said, tension in his voice.

My mother got up and faced her brother. Her red high-heeled patent leather sandals looked tacky next to his shabby and stained cowboy boots. The navy and red dress was damp and hung shapeless and wilted around her body. Even her permed hair was laid limp by the humidity. She turned and picked up the red purse that looked like a long envelope. Snapping it open, she pulled a few bills from her wallet and shoved them into Jando's shirt pocket. Then she placed her hand on his face, letting it linger for a few seconds before moving to her own face to wipe the tears sliding down her cheeks.

"*Cuídate, hermano. Que Dios te bendiga.*"

They hugged quickly and we stepped out the door. Uncle Jando's bony frame leaned against the door as he watched us step into the car. I waved, but his glistening eyes were looking far away, beyond the mountains.

In the front seat my mother's shoulders heaved quietly. Through the rearview mirror I saw dark clouds gathering over Batacosa. The driver pressed the gas pedal firmly, aiming the car straight ahead, to where the sky remained blue and the clouds white and billowy.

15

FIELD WORK

"EL FIEL'" WAS WHAT MY PARENTS CALLED IT—their Spanglish term
for the field. In an agricultural community, life revolves around
"the field." Whether they were conscious of the fact or not,
everyone had a stake in the land; it was the valley's very lifeline.
The farmers and farmworkers depended on the land for survival,
and the rest of the town relied on them to support the small
businesses that dotted the main street—all the grocery, hardware,
farming supply, and clothing stores.

For the farmer the field was a precious patch of land that,
given the right elements, weather, demand, and luck, determined
his livelihood. In turn, farmworker families like us became inex-
tricably tied to the grower's fate. Guided by the market, the
Farmer's Almanac, new farming methods, and their own gut
instinct, growers had to strategize: where and how much to plant
and when to rotate the crops. The wild card was the weather.
Not enough rain or too much rain could ruin the careful plant-
ing of the crops, and that could mean no work for Papá. But
predictable weather cycles brought abundance to the fields.

There was no overtime or time and a half on the farm. As
with most of the farmworkers, Papá's employment arrangement
was straightforward—you got paid for what you worked. Farm
labor provided no benefits, no health insurance, no medical or
pension plans, no guarantees. Many years later, after almost twenty
years of working for Don Ray, Papá was laid off with a hand-
shake and two weeks' pay. Don Ray, wealthier than he ever
dreamed, had decided to retire from farming.

If you were young and Mexican it was understood you would work in the fields. Even if you didn't want to, it was the only available summer work. My first time was when I was eleven.

I was bored and despondent. I wanted to go on vacation like so many of my classmates, but my parents couldn't afford it.

My mother was sympathetic; she was yearning to see Aunt Tere in Mexicali, who was having financial problems. One night Papá talked about the garlic field that was about to be harvested. Mamá had an idea. "*Viejo,* if Chelita and I picked garlic we could earn enough to go to Mexicali."

Papá looked dubious. He had made it clear to my mother that he didn't want her to work. "No one is going to say I can't support my family," he'd declared.

But Mamá persisted. "It's only for five days and it's right here on the farm."

"Please, Papá. I really want to go to Mexico!" I added.

Papá raised his hands up and laughed. *"Ya, ya, ándale, pues.* I'll talk to Don Ray." It was one of the few times he gave in so easily.

Don Ray was skeptical about employing us. He worried we might not have the stamina to earn our way. After all, this was a man's job and he had a deadline. What if we slowed things down and he had to keep another worker for an extra day?

"Since when is picking garlic such an art?" my mother snorted when my father told her about Don Ray's reservations.

"But," he continued, "he said he'd take a chance."

We started at 6 a.m. the next day. The August morning was cold and gray, still shrouded in damp fog. We wore layers of clothes—a T-shirt, a sweatshirt, a windbreaker—that would protect us from the early morning chill and could be discarded later when the afternoon sun got too hot. We wrapped scarves around our heads and topped them with knit caps. This was our field-work uniform, the same outfit you'll see men and women wearing today as you drive by California's valley fields.

A foreman demonstrated the proper way to pick garlic. "You hook your sack to this special belt. This frees your hands so you can pick the garlic and toss it into your sack."

We watched carefully as he attached the bag to his waist and sauntered down the row, stooping slightly, his hands whirling like a harvester machine, making garlic bulbs fly from the ground into the sack.

"Easy!" he said, straightening his back.

And it was—until the sack started getting full. Then it not only wouldn't stay on the belt hook, but it became nearly impossible for a skinny eleven-year-old to budge.

I spent the morning engineering ways to keep the bag around my waist. I tried belting it and looping it on different parts of my body with my scarf, but it was hopeless. At a certain fullness, the thing just couldn't be moved. I had to resort to a more laborious yet effective method. I'd drag the sack with both my hands, then run back and forth, picking handfuls of garlic and depositing them in the stationary bag. I must have looked as silly as a Keystone Cop.

I heard laughter echo from the nearby fields. I looked around, wondering what the joke was about, and slowly realized they were laughing at me! My stomach did a somersault when I heard the impatient crunch of the foreman's boots behind me. Was I going to be sent home?

"No, no, you don't do it right." He gestured wildly in front of me.

"But I can't do it the same way you do. The sack's too heavy," I tried to explain.

Then men's voices called out: "*¡Déjala, hombre!* Let the kid do it her way."

The foreman shrugged, rolled his eyes upward, and walked away, muttering under his breath, "Yeah, well, *he* wanted to hire them."

My mother walked toward me from another row smiling. It was lunch time.

After lunch, the afternoon sun slowed me down. Sweat trickled down my back, making me itchy and sticky. It was discouraging to see everyone passing me, row after row. Afternoon dragged on as heavy as the half-filled garlic sack I lugged. By the end of the day my shoulders felt as if someone had stuck a hot iron between them.

The days that followed were a blur of aching muscles and garlic bulbs. The rows seemed to stretch like rubber bands, expanding with each passing day. My mother's smile and words of encouragement—a salve the first few days—no longer soothed me. Even at home I felt overpowered by the insidious garlic. It permeated my skin and clothes. No matter how much I scrubbed, the garlic oozed from my pores, the odor nearly suffocating me in my sleep.

On what was to be the last morning, I tried to get out of bed but couldn't. My body was so sore that the slightest movement sent waves of pain through my muscles. My legs were rubbery from all the bending, and my shoulders felt as if they had been cleaved apart. My whole body was one throbbing ache. The field had defeated me.

"I just can't do it," I sobbed to my mother. The tears tasted like garlic.

"Anything worth having is worth working for," she said gently.

"I don't care about the vacation. I'm too tired. It's not worth it," I cried.

"There are only a few rows left. Are you sure you can't finish?" my mother persisted.

By then the few rows might as well have been hundreds to me. I felt bad about giving up after working so hard, but it just didn't seem fair to pay such a high price to go on vacation. After all, my classmates didn't have to.

My mother was quiet all day. I'd forgotten it was to have been her vacation too. When Papá came home his eyebrows shot up with surprise. There we were at home, sitting on the couch neatly dressed. He didn't change out of his work clothes right away but sat in the kitchen with his lunch pail still in his hands, listening to my mother's explanation. With the palm of his hand he shook the dust out of his hair and began speaking in his hesitant way. "Well. If we all pitch in...we can still finish up the rows tonight."

I looked at Papá's dust-rimmed, bloodshot eyes, his dusty hair and overalls. I knew by the slope of his shoulders he was tired from his own grueling fieldwork. A mixture of pity and gratitude overwhelmed me.

But I was torn. The thought of doing battle with the field again filled me with dread. I said nothing, swallowing my reluctance until it formed a lump in my throat.

That summer evening, the three of us worked side by side, teasing, talking, and laughing as we completed the task. By the time the last of the garlic sacks were lined up it was dusk and we had grown silent. The rosy glow from the setting sun made me feel warm, as did the relief of knowing the work was finally over and done.

Two days later we boarded the 9 p.m. southbound Greyhound bus. We left at night so we could sleep most of the journey, but of course it didn't quite work out that way.

The road stretched dark and long before us. San Lucas, San Ardo, San Miguel. My mother and I chatted quietly, our anticipation bubbling over like effervescence in a soft drink. The bus driver's chant of passing towns sounded like the faraway echo of an Indian prayer at sunset. Paso Robles, Atascadero, San Luis Obispo. For a long time we were able to keep sleep at arm's length, but soon the moon cast a hypnotic glow on the passing farm scenes, coaxing our eyes to close, the rhythmic hum of engine vibrations lulling us into a slumber. Along the trail the bus paused long enough to pick up an occasional night owl, but otherwise it remained luxuriously half empty, mercifully not stopping at every single waypoint on its milk-wagon route.

But there was no mercy in Santa Barbara. It was a mandatory break for the driver, so all sleepers were rudely roused. The rules were strict: no passengers in the bus while the driver was away.

So at 2 a.m. out we stumbled, squinting at the brightly lit Santa Barbara depot. We slouched over the Formica coffee shop counter, yawning miserably as we watched our bus driver consume a full-course dinner. Feeling nauseous, I looked away and saw the other passengers for the first time, mostly older Americans who kept to themselves.

Back on the bus, no sooner were our eyes at a drowsy half-mast than twilight dissolved over steely predawn Los Angeles, where we had to make another mandatory stop. Inside the depot people groaned as they learned of the three-hour layover before the departure of our connecting border bus.

We had been warned about the Los Angeles depot. Friends quoted stories from *La Opinión,* L.A.'s Spanish-language newspaper, about purse snatching and stabbings in the women's bathrooms. There lurked "bad" Mexicans, they said—evil, dangerous women easily recognized by orange beehive hairdos, short, tight skirts, and tattoos. They hid in depot stalls, stalking innocent, unsuspecting country bumpkins like us to rob. We were advised never to enter an empty bathroom or one occupied by anyone who looked like an East L.A. pachuca-type.

I saw my mother cross herself. She always crossed herself—before entering a car, when we passed a church, or even when she had a frightening thought. *"¡Ave María Purísima!"* she'd exclaim. This habit had started to embarrass me, but at the L.A. depot I welcomed it.

Once on the Calexico-bound bus we noticed the passengers were no longer older Americans but mostly Mexicans and their children. The sky's gray pallor had turned into a pretty pink blush, promising warmth and sunshine. Outside, the landscape changed from farms and green hills to palm trees and ocean vistas. Southern California's warm breath tickled the skin beneath my sweater.

Indio, Brawley, El Centro. We entered the Imperial Valley, where the land is parched and baked and mesquite mingles with date trees. Barefoot brown children and skinny dogs lazily looked up as the bus wound its way through small, dusty towns reminiscent of Mexico. Mexico was not far away now.

Chatter inside the bus reached a feverish pitch. Someone began singing *"Mexico Lindo y Querido"* as passengers cheered. The driver smiled, ignoring the rules against singing and playing radios.

Calexico—the end of the line, the last stop on the U.S. side. Mexicali was just across the border. Stepping off the cool bus, we were enveloped by the Baja California heat like logs in a fire. At 8 a.m. it was already 100 degrees.

Aunt Tere, Uncle Mario, and some of my cousins rushed forward to greet us. We did not tell them we picked garlic to get there. We did not speak of the hard work and the isolated lives we lived. My mother talked about the bountiful crops, the tomatoes she canned, and the jams she made. She promised to bring it all for them at Christmas.

16

TÍA TERE

EVERY YEAR RIGHT BEFORE SUMMER or winter vacation I'd ask Papá the same question: "When are we leaving for Mexico?"

And he'd always answer: *"¿Quién sabe?"*

In fact, we never really did know until that last moment how much time we could take, or if we would even be able to go. On the farm, vacations were dictated by weather conditions. They were a variable that always hung over our heads like a question mark.

Once Papá gave the word, however, my mother would go into overdrive, running around throwing things out of closets and drawers, complaining that he never gave her enough notice. How could she possibly pack for a vacation in two nights?

All year long my mother scoured sales, buying and stuffing away gifts for our relatives in Mexico. During the summer she canned vegetables, jams, and jellies. Bags of walnuts and almonds collected from trees on the farm, beans from the fall harvest, apples, used clothing from Don Ray's family, modest gifts bought on sale, and anything edible or useful she may have received during the year (she hardly ever kept anything for herself)—all this was methodically accumulated for her Mexican family.

The very last things to go into the car were our own suitcases and extra blankets and pillows. With six children, Aunt Tere never had enough blankets for her guests. With no heat in the house, we had learned to bring our own. My mother always "accidentally" left a blanket behind.

There was not a nook or cranny in that car that wasn't stuffed. We resembled a prosperous Joad family. I would have died of embarrassment if any of my school friends had caught a glimpse of me tucked in among the bags and pillows, but I didn't have to worry about that. We hit the road at 4 a.m. in order to be in Mexicali by early evening.

I loved these road trips more than anything else. They filled me with an intoxicating sense of freedom and discovery. On the road we had no social stigma. We weren't just farmworkers or Mexicans—we were travelers, recognized as a special group by the gas station attendants, mom-and-pop restaurant owners, and motel clerks. Road travel changed Papá too. His personality transformed. He shed the veneer of moodiness and impatience and became ebullient. Unfortunately, it changed my mother too. Car trips made her nervous and tense. She had a hard time relaxing enough to enjoy the total experience. This sense of journey, of lightness, was shared only by Papá and me. Whether speeding on a freeway outside of Los Angeles or cruising through the date farms in Indio, we were kindred spirits. It was on a California highway that the two of us didn't need words to communicate our joy at being together unconstrained. I only wished he could always be like his road personality.

Arriving in Mexicali we were greeted with great whoops of joy from the cousins. My mother and her sister would welcome each other with a joke and then dissolve into tears.

Year after year, whether winter or summer, this same scene would be repeated. Only each year it was in a different house, in a poorer neighborhood.

When my parents married, Aunt Tere and Uncle Mario were enjoying an upper-middle-class lifestyle. They attended fancy parties, entertained socially prominent friends, had servants, and even vacationed in places like Las Vegas and San Francisco.

"I'm sorry, María Luisa, we didn't have enough time to stop and see you," was Aunt Tere's explanation when my mother found out they'd rented a car in San Francisco to visit Carmel. My mother was hurt. My mother suspected Aunt Tere did not want her friends from *la sociedad* to know we were farmworkers.

She told them we lived in San Francisco, not King City, a lie my mother perpetuated.

It was a complicated social situation. Although my mother was not ashamed of her life in the United States, there was a strong stigma against the people—mostly dark-skinned Indians—who left Mexico to find work in the fields, an opportunity ten times better than their prospects in Mexico. *La sociedad* regarded these poor Mexicans with no family background or connections as inferior. Not even a changed passport or money would alter their mindset. As the ruling class in Mexico, *la sociedad* defines social rules, runs the country, sets the moral tone. The middle class eagerly plays by the same rules. Sometimes even the genteel poor can be participants, as long as a family can prove the right ancestry and connections. My mother chose not to complicate the situation. Our time there was too short.

Aunt Tere was drawn to society and material trappings. She liked to say she appreciated quality and class. She never shopped in Mexicali, only in Calexico at the Sam Ellis store. She collected crystal vases, ashtrays, and bowls. She was the sister who had opposed my mother's divorce on the grounds that it would make the family look bad to the neighbors.

Tall, thin doctors' and businessmen's wives were her friends. They'd come pick her up for canasta games and lunches in two-piece suits, and pointy high-heeled shoes with matching envelope-style purses. They wore their hair piled on the tops of their heads or teased into smooth pageboys—poufed out imitations of Jackie Kennedy's look. Amid a clutter of high heels and breathless chatter, they'd casually pull on their enormous dark glasses before leaving in a cloud of imported perfume.

My mother would not go on this outings. She was suspicious of the ladies from *la sociedad*. "Don't believe they're truly your friends," she warned Aunt Tere. "Have fun with them, but don't get hurt."

"*Ay,* María Luisa, you're not jealous, are you?"

Stung, my mother just shook her head.

These friendships were put to the test when my uncle lost his job. Money went missing from the company he worked for and, as the controller, he was the prime suspect. Although he discovered later it was one of the managers, he held his tongue because the man was an old friend, the one who'd helped him get his job in the first place, and their wives were intimates. Uncle Mario tried to cover for him and wound up being fired himself.

"Don't worry, Mario," the friend promised. "I'll never forget what you did for me. I'll find you another position."

But he didn't. My uncle was thrown into a five-year downward spiral during which he alternated between low-paying jobs and unemployment. They slowly sold off their luxuries—crystal, silver, jewelry. Their "friends" helped them by buying their nicest items. But eventually the friends disappeared and they lost their place in *la sociedad*.

Back on the farm in King City, my mother spent a lot of time thinking about life's unfair treatment of her sister.

"Mi pobre hermana," my mother sighed, her eyes misty with tears. "She suffers so much."

After the economic free fall Aunt Tere was diagnosed with diabetes. Depression, stress, and not following a prescribed medical routine transformed her into a semi-invalid. On our trips to visit her, we never knew if we'd find her in bed moaning or up and about. She suffered extreme mood swings and a constant series of ailments, ranging from stomachaches to migraines.

"Tere, you must take medicine and follow a special diet," my mother pleaded.

"And what do I buy it with? And who will cook for me?" Aunt Tere would lament, lifting her head from her pillow and gesturing to her six rowdy children.

There were many disappointments, shattered dreams, joys, and ironies I never knew about, I'm sure. They were kept locked in the inner sanctum that was my aunt's bedroom. Here all my mother's sisters gathered with other female friends and relatives to unburden themselves. From behind those closed doors my cousins and I would hear impassioned whispers, raucous laughter, and soul-cleansing sobs. As young children, these sounds frightened us and made our imaginations race with fearful speculation. But the women always emerged from these tribal rites relaxed and refreshed.

During one of Uncle Mario's employment droughts Papá took a couple of days off during the summer to take the family every kind of food and fruit we could load in the car because my mother feared they were starving.

"Teresa, have Mario come back with us. The tomato picking season is about to start. He can make some dollars to tide you over until he finds a job."

Aunt Tere was appalled. "Mario *es un profesional*. It would demoralize him to work the field."

A week after we returned home we received a letter from Aunt Tere announcing she was arriving that same week with my twelve-year-old cousin Blanca to work in the tomato fields.

"That's absurd!" my mother cried. "She's a sick woman. How can that *huevón* allow her to do this!"

For years my mother had longed for Aunt Tere to visit, but now, under these circumstances, she looked forward to their arrival with apprehension instead of joy.

"I'm fine, María Luisa," Aunt Tere insisted. "That's why I came. I thought a change of scenery would do me good and well, you know, we could use a few dollars."

I looked at my aunt, pale and delicate, her hair newly colored ash blonde, and then at my cousin, short for her age, small-boned and frail. I couldn't imagine them in the field! Although my mother and I had never picked tomatoes, I knew we were stronger and more robust than these two.

Once again Papá cleared the four of us to work with Don Ray. Unlike in the garlic harvest, we weren't the only women on the crew. Entire families with children of all ages out of school for the summer worked in units, filling boxes of tomatoes.

I was excited to see many kids near my age and imagined befriending them. This would make the days seem shorter. But I was disappointed right away when I realized that the tomato picking families were all business, aloof, working only together like a well-drilled team, rarely speaking or, when they did, only to each other.

My cousin started whining the first day.

"My poor baby. Now, you take a break whenever you get tired," Aunt Tere cooed at Blanca.

Blanca's rest periods got longer and longer as the week moved on. When she was working she'd pick one tomato at a time and stroll slowly back and forth to dump it in the wooden box. She'd complain about the heat, the dust, or the tomato plants that made her itch. Or she'd take one or two bites out of the plumpest, juiciest tomato she could find and then discard it.

"Mamá, she's getting away without working!" I complained to my mother.

"She's not helping her mother at all. But you are, *mi'jita*. You're a very responsible worker. You are a great help to me," my mother said.

Her praise encouraged me to work faster and harder. I felt competitive with my cousin. Because we were the closest in age we were always being compared: who got better grades, was good in games, could sing better. Blanca usually won out. By picking more tomatoes than her, though, I'd be superior at something. Besides, picking tomatoes was not as grueling as garlic. For one thing there was no sack to drag around. Once your boxes were full, one of the men would stack them for you, marking your number with chalk. At the end of the day, when the boxes were tallied, your pay was determined by the number of boxes. It was rumored that some unscrupulous workers filled the bottoms of boxes with rocks and layered the tops with tomatoes. The foreman used that example to issue a warning that individuals resorting to fraud would be blackballed from ever working in any field in California. We believed him!

My aunt began to fade around the third day. First she wanted to know where the bathroom was. In the early sixties, bathrooms were not provided for fieldworkers. If you had to go, you went behind the bushes. Aunt Tere said it was inhuman and indecent.

"I'm not going squat like an Indian woman and have some man looking at my *nalgas!*"

What she did instead was drive the car all the way to our house and back (a twenty-minute ride, roundtrip) whenever she had to go to the bathroom. My mother pursed her lips but said nothing. Aunt Tere probably would have continued doing this had the foreman not caught her one day and demanded she pee in the bushes like everyone else.

"Well, Teresa, now you have to show your *nalgas* just like the rest of us," my mother teased. Aunt Tere answered with a glare.

The tomato picking was scheduled for about twelve days. By day six, Blanca had given up and stayed home. On day eight Aunt Tere joined her. But my mother and I forged forward.

On the very last day, they showed up early to collect their pay, and then decided to leave for Mexico that very afternoon. We were in another part of the tomato field when we saw them talking to the foreman and receive their pay.

When we returned home, we said our good-byes and off they went with Papá to the bus depot. My mother gave a deep sigh of relief and sat down. We were both glad they were gone. Their time with us had been more strained than uplifting. For the first time in days, I saw my mother relax, a look of satisfaction softening her face.

"I haven't even opened our paycheck," she smiled, standing up. I had been promised some of the money to do with as I wanted, and I squirmed in my seat with anticipation.

My mother's face turned white, then red. "Oh, no! We've been shortchanged!"

She told Papá the minute he walked into the house that night. But the foreman told him there was no mistake.

"Your wife's sister said to divide all the boxes evenly between the two of them," the foreman explained.

At first my mother was furious. But then she considered that it could be a misunderstanding. Maybe she hadn't made herself clear. Time passed and the more my mother talked it out, the more she rationalized the whole episode. I thought the evidence weighed against Aunt Tere.

"They cheated us and got away with it, just like Blanca got away with not working," I said scornfully.

"You must be more compassionate, *hija*. Things are not always what they seem."

By the time we saw each other again at Christmas, I felt guilty that I had thought badly of them. Their neediness appalled me. When we arrived, they'd descended upon us like locusts and picked the car clean. No matter how much we brought, it was never enough. They were like baby birds, mouths open, constantly needing feedings. I saw my mother slip a bill here or bill there in her sister's or brother's pockets.

But even during those lean years, my aunt always found a way to give me a little *cariño,* as she called it. My first piece of jewelry, a gold bracelet, came from her. Another time a beautiful sweater and my first bottle of cologne, L'Air Du Temps. How did she manage it? The Corral sisters had learned to be resourceful. They had to for their family's sake. It was a lesson that did not escape me.

17

BORDER COUSINS

THEY INTRODUCED ME AS "LA PRIMA AMERICANA," even though
I was Mexican-born and -bred, just like them. But the way
they saw it, I was American. Not only did I live in the United
States, but I was light-skinned, *güera*.

My six cousins—four boys and two girls—were various
shades of brown, Hector being the darkest. My Aunt Tere
called him her handsome *negro*, "a Mexican Nat King Cole."

The boys traveled together like a pack of skinny, brown-
legged, crew-cut-topped young animals. They appeared and
disappeared in and out of rooms in a whirling din of motion
and noise. At first glance, the girls seemed placid and calm.
Feminine creatures in flouncy dresses whose doe-eyed expressions masked their terrorists tendencies, they dominated their
brothers and the entire neighborhood. Those sweet little girls
were capable of incredible strength, armwrestling their brothers into submission and knowing what areas of the human
body—when squeezed just so—could cause paralyzing pain.
Boy, I admired them!

"Aren't those girls a little wild?" my mother asked after wit-
nessing yet another display of their Amazon power.

"If they don't take care of themselves, the boys will walk all
over them," my aunt answered nonchalantly.

When they banded together, my cousins could be quite for-
midable and intimidating. They had a reputation in the family
for their clannishness and for the dangerous pranks they played
on visiting cousins. I, however, was given the opportunity to

earn a place in their tribe because they admired the United States. Of course, along the way I did have to pass "tests," like playing chicken in dense traffic and joining games of let's-see-who-can-pass-out-first-in-a-closed-up-car in 120 degree weather.

It was the decade of the television cowboy in Mexico as well as the United States, and my cousins and their friends avidly watched every dubbed Western sandwiched between *novelas* on Mexican TV. They all agreed the best clothes were American and raved about American food like pancakes, hamburgers, and banana splits.

"Are you really American?" my cousins' friends would ask.

"*¡Simón, es gringa!*" a cousin would respond proprietarily. "She eats hamburgers all the time, don't you?"

"All the time—and root beer, too," I'd add for good measure, remembering my schoolmates back home talking a lot about the A&W brand. The truth was, I never ate hamburgers. Nor had I ever tasted root beer. My mother didn't like making hamburgers and neither of my parents even knew what root beer was. "Your friends drink beer?" was their horrified reaction.

It was great to be popular in Mexico by acting out being an American, because in the United States I certainly didn't feel like one.

But the mania for all things American diminished soon after President John F. Kennedy was assassinated. During that year's Christmas visit, my cousins were decidedly cool. Americans, they said, were murderers. They killed their own president. Mexico loved the Kennedys, especially John Kennedy and his beautiful wife Jacqueline, who spoke to the Mexican people in their own language during a diplomatic trip. Americans were appalled by the killing, but Mexicans were sickened.

From then on, through the rest of my adolescence, I was put on the defensive and had to participate in endless debates about the merits of the United States versus Mexico. The discussions revolved around questions like: "Who has more criminals, the United States or Mexico?" "Who's a better singer, Elvis Presley or Enrique Guzmán?" or "Who was a better President, Benito Juárez or George Washington?" I recall coming close to winning the best-president debate, but I definitively lost the other two. My cousins persuaded me that the United States must have more criminals because we had to have the electric chair and Guzmán could hold notes longer than Elvis. In the end, the discussions were actually useful. They sharpened our verbal skills and in a roundabout way taught us about both countries.

My cousins really didn't know very much about the United States, even though they lived just across the border. Calexico on the American side wasn't the "real" United States to them, much in the way Americans feel Tijuana isn't the "real" Mexico. In Calexico just about everybody was Mexican anyway, and aside from a few store clerks, immigration officers at the border, and the pharmacist at Thrifty, Americans were downright scarce. I recall the excitement surrounding towheaded Anglo children in the markets. Real Americans!

Two of my cousins did manage to visit us in the Salinas Valley—the real United States—for extended periods of time. Mario came to work and Blanca to study. They did not enjoy their visits. My handsome cousin Mario, a heartbreaker in Mexico, couldn't understand why *gringas* didn't respond to his flirting or why it embarrassed me to death. Blanca resented the condescending manner people sometimes took with her. Once in a store I noticed she was having difficulty getting assistance from a clerk. I knew the clerk slightly and translated for her, adding, "She's my cousin." The clerk raised an eyebrow and apologized: "Oh, I'm sorry. I thought she was one of the field Mexicans."

My cousins found this prejudice bewildering. The border town had shielded them from this cultural peculiarity, and their exposure to Americans visiting Mexico had been pleasant. Those Americans found Mexicans in Mexico charming, but Mexicans, it seemed, quickly lost their "charm" once in the United States. My cousins were proud, and being snubbed left them with little desire to explore beyond the small-town prejudices. They did not return.

18

CHRISTMAS IN MEXICO

AS YEARS WENT BY, it became increasingly difficult for Papá to take summer vacations, but we continued to visit Mexico faithfully every Christmas. In my reality, Mexico and family were synonymous with Christmas, and more than anything else in my childhood, I looked forward to spending the holiday with my cousins. Like thousands of other immigrants, we were part of the yearly family pilgrimage that continues today.

My parents, who grew up in Mexico, felt awkward imitating American holiday traditions. They were appalled by the mistletoe custom, disliked the taste of eggnog (they thought it a poor substitute for *rompope*), and snickered at Rudolph the Red-Nosed Reindeer and Frosty the Snowman. Nostalgically they spoke of *posadas*, elaborate créches, and *los Tres Reyes Magos*—the Three Wise Men.

We felt detached from American celebrations but, like polite guests, we'd sample the traditions—hum the carols, admire the ornate decorations glowing around houses at night, bake the cookies—but with great restraint. We were waiting to fill our hunger for celebration until we got to Mexico.

Our reward was the family. For my parents, it was an opportunity to have meaningful conversations, to gossip and share joys and sorrows. For me, an only child, it was wonderful to roam the neighborhood with a pack of cousins, fighting, playing, and defending each other from bullies. It filled the emptiness created by my psychological isolation in American culture and the physical isolation that came from living on a remote farm.

And then there were all the parties! Bazaars at the church, *posadas* in neighbors' homes. Refreshments included steaming dark

Mexican chocolate with fragrant cinnamon sticks, freshly baked, plump tamales, *churros,* and *buñuelos.*

As in a musical comedy, songs arose out of the blue in the form of a musician with a guitar, a record player, a radio, or a capella singing among adults.

On Christmas Eve, my aunt prepared the family feast. She cooked all day and laid out a sumptuous buffet on a white table-cloth embroidered with large red poinsettias. Friends and neighbors dropped by all night and we took turns touring the neighborhood, returning to compare notes on ambience and food.

At 11:30 p.m., everyone joined the parade of neighbors going to *misa de gallo,* midnight mass. The church filled up and crowds spilled into the streets. My cousins and I sleepily propped each other up, alert only to the sweet smell of frankincense and the high notes sung by the choir.

After mass we crawled into bed, exhausted and cold but anxious to open our modest presents in the morning.

The celebrations continued through New Year's Eve, the night we all stayed up, even the very youngest cousin, to greet the new year with tears and hugs for good luck.

Volleys of fireworks exploded throughout the city, and we joined in until our bag of red firecrackers was empty and our noses were burning from the smell of sulfur. We'd run home where the adults were already having hot, steaming bowls of *menudo.*

I loved these Mexican holidays—the nonstop partying, the food, the cousins, the family, the warmth and sharing.

But one year, the year it rained and rained, my father didn't say, "Ok, pack up." A season of rain meant he couldn't work in the fields laying down irrigation pipes. Rain meant he couldn't drive the tractor to make those neat, long rows. Rain meant no money for Christmas in Mexico.

Everyone shared the disappointment. My mother didn't even want to buy a tree, but she did—a little raggedy pine, for me. And on Christmas morning there were three presents under the tree, all for me.

We never missed another Christmas in Mexico after that, even if it meant, as my mother said, *con sacrificios.*

The author's great-grandfather, Nepomuceno Corral (far right), his
son Adolfo, and Adolfo's wife and daughters at the family home
in Batacosa, Sonora, 1900s.

The author, 18 months old.

The author, 3 years old in a *china poblana* costume,
Nogales, Mexico.

Tito del Castillo. Photo given to the author's mother during their courtship in the late 1940s.

The author and her mother,
passport photo for California
trip, 1957.

José García and María Luisa before their marriage
in Mexico, late 1950s.

The author, 6 years old, in King City.

The author's first-grade
photo, 7 years old.

The author in the farmhouse
on Jolon Road, 8 years old.

Mrs. Laura Rojas's fourth-grade class at San Lorenzo
Elementary School, 1961.

The author with her parents,
celebrating First Communion.

The author, 14 years old, outside the *casa grande*.

The author interning
at the *King City Rustler Herald*
newspaper, 1970.

The author's high school graduation photo, 1970.

19

A Teacher Who Mattered

THAT MRS. ROJAS WAS THE MEANEST TEACHER in the entire school was widely accepted as fact. She was not only strict but also cold-blooded. It was whispered that in her bottom desk drawer she kept a thick wooden paddle—a paddle that grew with each retelling—and she used it capriciously and frequently. I entered the fourth grade filled with apprehension.

But sitting in her class the first day of school, I found it difficult to imagine the diminutive woman as the terror of San Lorenzo Elementary School. She must have been in her late fifties. Short and plump, she wore her gray-streaked hair in a coiled braid around her head, adorned with Spanish combs, her one pretension. Her wardrobe consisted of pleated skirts topped with long, colorful vests. The look was decidedly ethnic at a time when ethnic was not chic.

Laura Rojas was the sole Mexican American teacher in the agricultural town where I grew up, a town where the number of Mexican kids steadily increased with the years.

She set high standards for both Anglos and Mexicans; she never played favorites. But long before the 1980s were declared "the decade of the Hispanic," Mrs. Rojas made being Mexican a yearlong celebration. Mrs. Rojas sneaked into the classroom important cultural lessons influencing our perceptions of Latinos. Ours was the only class to have Spanish language lessons. Once a week we memorized Mexican folk songs and practiced the alphabet. She wove Spanish and Mexican history, art, and literature into our curriculum. On our annual field trip, she took us to San Antonio Mission, explaining which traditions were brought by the local Jolon Indians, the missionaries, and the early Mexican settlers.

During Christmas break, Mrs. Rojas vacationed in Mexico City and Acapulco, and she brought back souvenirs—things ten-year-olds are impressed by: a jeweled beetle pin and a handful of jumping beans. She encouraged the kids to bring their own Mexican souvenirs for Show and Tell. Surprisingly, it was the Anglos who showed up with pottery, sombreros, sarapes, and onyx figurines. The Mexican children looked around embarrassed, empty-handed. We didn't realize our everyday home objects were "souvenirs."

One of the most memorable episodes during my years in Mrs. Rojas's class was the day our class picture was taken and Mrs. Rojas announced that the prettiest and most photogenic person in class was Ramona—a shy Mexican girl. The blondes were shocked, Ramona blossomed with new self-confidence, and the rest of us were struck by the notion that a Mexican could be considered beautiful.

But as delightful and nurturing as Mrs. Rojas was, she was also stern. True to the rumors, the paddle did indeed come down on anyone who didn't abide by her rules, including two Mexican girls who made the mistake of brawling at noontime.

In the decades since fourth grade, I've thought about Laura Rojas often, as one remembers teachers who have made a difference. I didn't earn the best grades that year. I didn't discover any particular talents, and I wasn't the teacher's pet. She was not my role model; non-Latinos would later occupy that place. What Mrs. Rojas gave me was something more intangible. The seeds of self-worth, acceptance, and pride in who I was were planted so subtly that I didn't even realize they were growing until many years later, when I found them rooted inside me.

The last time I saw Laura Rojas was one winter afternoon in the late sixties. I was a teenager and had made it a practice to occasionally visit my old fourth-grade teacher. That day I went to brag about winning a writing award. I wanted to be a writer, I told her, and would start by writing her story.

She looked old and ill, but her drawn face brightened. Matching my bravado, she leaned toward me and said, "And I have a very interesting life to tell."

As the warm afternoon shadows lengthened into darkness, she fixed her eyes on a faraway object and began her story.

She was the first in her family to finish school, to go to college. Her parents were too poor to help with expenses, and her grades didn't merit a scholarship, so she worked summers and during the school year to pay her way—propelled by a drive to teach, especially young Mexican children. "I wanted to show the world that a Mexican could be a teacher, and darned good one."

Her eyes lost their stony focus as she related long-buried emotions.

"The humiliations I suffered were very painful," she said softly.

She was the only Mexican in an agricultural college where Mexicans were treated as inferiors. Girls in cashmere sweaters and pearls called her "the Mexican maid" because she was a cafeteria worker, and they wondered out loud "when the college started letting in braceros."

For Laura, college was years of hardship, loneliness, and deprivation. "But it was all worth it. Those girls...most of them dropped out of school to get married. I became a teacher. And a respected one. I've loved every minute."

I never heard about the rest of her life—her marriage, her travels, her children or grandchildren—as she died shortly after that conversation. I've never been able to tell her story, until now.

20

BILLIE

SEVEN YEARS AFTER WE MOVED to the farm on Jolon Road, we found ourselves alone. The farmworkers were gone and their housing dismantled. After a number of successful crops, the boss and his family moved into town, where they'd bought an impressive ranch-style house with a billiard room and a lanai and a living room decorated all in red.

We also moved up. Into the boss's old house, *la casa grande*.

We hadn't counted on the utter stony silence and isolation of being the only three human beings left on the farm. Sometimes the only sound we heard was the wind whistling through the eucalyptus trees.

"My God. If someone killed us, no one would know for days!" My mother's comment sent a chill down my spine.

We were so lonely, my mother was downright gleeful with the arrival of a wayward Fuller Brush man. She always bought something just to encourage repeat visits. And she never shut the door on the Jehovah's Witnesses that found their way up our bumpy road. She respectfully listened to their words and kindly dismissed them by buying a *Watchtower* or two for a dime, ensuring they would, at some point, return.

That's why I was filled with excitement when I saw the rustling of curtains in the *casa chica*, our old home, as I walked from the school bus stop one afternoon.

At thirteen, the single most important thing missing from my life was a friend. I had school friends but no confidante, no one whose parents would drive back and forth into the country on the weekends, no one who wouldn't mind too much that my mother couldn't communicate with her mother since she had not learned English, having lived on the farm all these years. I held hope that whoever had moved in might have a daughter close to my age who could become a friend.

I restrained myself from running over to find out until the weekend.

Saturday arrived all gold and orange. The autumn sun dappled the outside with a warm glow. I kicked the leaves along the path as I headed over to visit the new neighbor, carrying a jar of homemade jam my mother had insisted I take.

The house was an old friend, as familiar as my room. I knocked lightly on the faded white door and held my breath.

"Hey there!" a freckle-faced young girl greeted me.

My eyes widened in amazement. She was as thin and tall as a cattail except for what looked like a volleyball around her middle. Her dirty blonde hair hung straight to her shoulders. She stood grinning a big, toothy smile that softened her sharp features and gave her hollow cheeks a rounder look.

"You must be the neighbor gal. I've been meaning to visit with you. But I've been feeling a little poorly. I get this morning sickness all day long!" She patted her stomach meaningfully.

"Here's something for you. My mother sent it."

"Oh, my goodness gracious! Ain't that just so nice. Did your mama make this? My granny used to can every summer, too. I helped her. She showed me how to do lots of things, but I'm so dumb. All I learned to make was biscuits. And a little bit of sewing. I sewed this top. Do you like it?"

"It's really pretty," I politely agreed. I really thought it was thin and faded.

"Shoot, I haven't even asked you to come in and sit down. Where are your manners, Billie? Oh! That's my name—Billie." She giggled as if she had just told a funny story. "You know, I've been here only a few days but I've been so lonesome. Doncha just get so lonesome out here? I'm glad you came over. Now I can have someone to talk to!"

Billie was a nonstop talker, but her chatter didn't bother me; it filled the farm's silence and void. It was going to be fun having her as a neighbor.

I learned more about Billie and her husband, Jacky, from my father that night.

"That boy is green and lazy. This is his third job in three months. Don Ray must have felt sorry for him and given him a chance. The boy practically begged for the job. Seems the wife is expecting."

"And she's so young," my mother added.

"He worked for Johnson over in San Lucas. Margarito says the boy has a liquor problem." He gestured, tipping his thumb toward his mouth.

After my father left the kitchen to watch his Saturday night TV boxing match, my mother turned to me and said, "It's a good thing for you to visit Billie. She needs a friend."

It was easy to fall into a pattern of stopping by Billie's house as often as I could. She was easygoing and fun to be with. We discovered we both hated snotty girls, liked mushy movies, and wished our hair were curly. I talked to her about books I was reading (*Wuthering Heights,* Jane Austen), and she told me about TV shows she watched when she lived with her family.

My mother always sent something along, a jar of preserves, a bag of walnuts, or tortillas. When Billie opened her refrigerator to put away our offerings, I noticed it was all but empty. Often there was only milk and beer. It struck me as odd, but when I told my mother she only shook her head and set her mouth in a straight line.

One day a few weeks after they had moved in, Billie greeted me literally hopping with excitement the moment I stepped in the door.

"Look! Look! See anything different?"

I looked around the small living room taking inventory: two wooden chairs with paint peeling on the legs, one orange crate that doubled as a table, and a lumpy, cat-clawed easy chair.

Before my eyes finished sweeping the room Billie squealed, "It's a TV! Jacky got us a TV! Isn't he just the sweetest man you ever heard of? Now I can watch *American Bandstand*. Heck! We can watch it together." Her green eyes danced with joy.

I didn't see what the big deal was. I often invited Billie over to my house to watch TV, but she always found a way not to say either "yes" or "no." She'd nod noncommittally and then she was off on another subject. Now she was bragging about her TV.

I decided it didn't matter whose TV we watched, just as long as we could watch *American Bandstand* together.

"Jacky and I used to dance together all the time we was dating. Oh, he'd dance so close and slow. Just like that couple is doing."

"I thought you said you didn't go to school dances because the kids were snotty?"

"Heck, no. He'd come over to my house after school and we'd put on records and dance. Ma and Pa were at work and just the younger kids were at home, but they didn't bother us none."

"How old were you when you started dating Jacky?"

"I noticed him when I was thirteen, but I was a skinny little kid and he didn't take no notice. So I guess I was fourteen when he finally liked me. And here I am just turned sixteen and a married woman. Just like a fairy tale!" Billie wriggled her left hand, showing off the gold ring that left a green stain around her third finger.

"Gee, Billie, I can't imagine being pregnant at fifteen," I said. But what I really wanted to say was that I couldn't imagine kids only two years older than I "doing it."

My mother and I had never had "the talk." In Mexico, that was reserved for the day before your wedding night. But the sophisticated fourteen-year-old niece of one of my mother's friends had set me straight awhile back. She had several married sisters, so she *knew*.

A dreamy look came into Billie's eyes. "You just don't know how good being in love feels." She leaned back against her chair, then straightened up tall. "Being in love means you want some-one so bad it hurts. It hurts so bad you wouldn't care if your arm got torn off if that's what it takes to show your love."

The passion in her voice made me feel uncomfortable and embarrassed for her. What she described didn't sound like any-thing I'd ever read or what my mother described as her romances. Yet it was strangely exciting in a disquieting kind of way. I had not met Jacky and imagined him slender and dark with languid eyes. Someone who could stir a girl to the kind of emotion Billie displayed. Mentally I reviewed the boys at school I'd had crushes on. I couldn't possibly imagine wanting to cut off my arm for any of them.

A sharp rap on the door broke into my thoughts. We looked at each other in surprise.

"*Hola,* Billie." It was my mother. "Tell her I brought them dinner tonight so she won't have to cook," my mother said to me in Spanish, holding out a platter of enchiladas, beans, and rice.

Billie clapped her hands gleefully as my mother carried the plate into the kitchen and opened the refrigerator door.

"Billie, you no milk. No milk, no eggs—*no hay comida!*" she said, throwing her hands up in the air.

"Yes, ma'am, it's because Jacky hasn't had time to go into town to take me grocery shopping. We're going tonight, ma'am. Soon as he comes home," Billie said, blushing to the roots of her hair.

"Billie, you have to eat for baby. *Importante* for baby," my mother insisted.

"Oh, don't worry about me, ma'am."

My mother patted Billie's cheek. "*Sí, sí,*" she nodded soothingly. To me she said, "Come home soon. It's almost time for dinner."

When she left, Billie sat down heavily. "Poor Jacky, he just works so hard. He's worn out every night. All he can do is fall asleep in front of the TV. Why, the poor man sometimes don't even eat dinner."

The front door swung open then.

"Jacky!"

"Hi, baby." Jacky mumbled the words through a dangling cigarette between chapped lips. I stared in shock. His skin was sallow and pimply, his yellow hair coarse and disheveled like hay before baling. As he took the cigarette out of his mouth, I noticed his fingers were stained a brownish-yellow. Only his eyes stood out, small and black like two ticks on a dog's teats. He looked about seventeen or eighteen.

Billie's face lit up as she ran to him and grabbed his arm. "This here's the neighbor gal that visits with me." She slid her arm around his skinny middle and he draped an arm possessively on her shoulders.

"H-h-hi," I stammered. "I was just leaving."

That night at dinner, Papá told us things weren't looking good for Jacky. He said Don Ray was tired of Jacky's being late every day and of his irresponsibility. "One Mexican worker is worth two of these Okies," Don Ray had said. My father chuckled as he related the story. I could tell he didn't like Jacky. He resented having to redo much of Jacky's work. Still, Don Ray wanted to give Jacky more time.

"If he were Mexican, he'd be long gone. But Okies, they get more slack," Papá grumbled.

Billie was getting rounder and rounder. If she knew anything was wrong with Jacky's work, she made no mention of it to me, but I noticed as the weather turned colder and we got closer to winter and Christmas, her mood seemed somber.

One chilly afternoon I knocked on Billie's door as usual. After no answer, I knocked again and then almost left, thinking Billie was out, before I heard shuffling footsteps and then the doorknob turn. She opened the door silently, not with her usual "Hiya!" Her swollen body moved listlessly away from me as if in slow motion. She gave me a wan smile as she sank into a chair and faced me fully. My stomach lurched. One side of her face was black and blue.

"You can't stay long today," she said quietly. "Jacky's kind of mad at your Pa for riding him on the job. He says he don't want no Mexican food or people in his house. I'm real sorry."

"But you and I are friends, Billie."

"You and your Mama are about the nicest people I ever met, okay? But I can't cross Jacky. He's my husband."

"Billie, what happened to your face?" I finally blurted out.

"Oh, this is nothing. It's my own doing. You know I just can't keep my mouth shut when I should. I just go on and on. My Papa used to slap me and say, 'Girl, you just don't know when to stop, do you?'" Her lower lip trembled and she bit into it to stop. "Jacky, he's so tired every night. He just works so hard. It's nothing, okay?"

A wave of nausea overtook me. The dingy room revolved around me, stuffy and suffocating.

Billie started crying softly, then in big gulps. "We don't have a Christmas tree for the baby," she sobbed.

"I have to go, Billie" was all I could say. I didn't know what to do.

I didn't say anything to my mother about the bruises. I didn't know what she would think. I just knew I didn't want her to think badly of Billie.

The next day I was surprised to find my mother standing on the front steps waiting for me after school.

"Did Billie have her baby?" I asked breathlessly.

"Billie and her husband are gone," she said quietly. "They left last night without giving notice."

"Oh" was all I managed to say.

I watched *American Bandstand* by myself that afternoon, but I wasn't really interested. After the show, I walked outside and rode my old bicycle aimlessly around the farm. Mixed emotions of anger, relief, and confusion battled within me. Pointing my bike toward the *casa chica,* I pedaled slowly. I sat looking into the windows for awhile, then walked up to the front door as if to visit Billie. I opened the door. The TV was gone. Ashtrays filled with Jacky's cigarette butts overflowed on the orange crate table. I walked into the kitchen, then into their bedroom. A steel-framed bed sat in the middle of the room covered with a bare, stained mattress. The empty house was so cold that I shivered. Before I left I took one last look at the room where I'd spent so many happy afternoons with Billie. I didn't know what I was looking for or what I expected to see. I only knew Billie had come close to being the friend I had longed for on the farm.

Shadows lengthened in the room, creating a forlorn and sad tableau. I turned and closed the door tight and headed quickly home through the chilly dusk.

21

DISAPPOINTMENTS

THE TEDIUM OF FARM LIFE became increasingly difficult for my mother. For a gregarious woman who thrived on people and conversation, it must have felt terribly confining. She was trapped.

She had never learned to drive a car. Papá had promised he would teach her, but he lacked patience as an instructor. Then, after she drove the car into a ditch during their short-lived lessons, she got spooked and was afraid to take the wheel. She would have tried again, she told me, but there was no one she could implore for lessons and there weren't any driving schools in King City.

After eight years in the United States, she still had not learned to speak English. She spoke Spanish to us on a daily basis, listened to Spanish radio stations, and used me as her personal translator whenever we went into town to go shopping or pay bills—a role I hated because she made me say things I found embarrassing, like paying compliments to store clerks or asking for lengthy explanations about bills at the PG&E office. She had picked up a few phrases and key words from watching television and knew just enough to get the gist of a conversation, but not enough to be conversant. Had we stayed in town, she would have had more opportunities to interact with the English-speaking community and even attended some of the first English-language night classes for adults.

She tried to go into town on a monthly basis, spending a day visiting friends, paying bills, or running errands. Because we didn't have a telephone, she'd show up on her friends' steps at noon and hope they were in the mood for a long afternoon visit. Papá would take her during his lunch hour and pick us up after work. Sometimes they'd be pleased to see her and other times they'd act put out, sitting there with a stony face when I arrived after school.

Occasionally, she'd tell me to meet her at one lady's house and when I'd show up she wouldn't be there; the person had either not been in the mood to visit or simply wasn't around. I'd have to wander to different houses to find her.

Estela was the most accommodating and understanding of her friends. She was in her sixties and had a taciturn demeanor. My mother was her opposite: talkative, witty, and cheerful. My mother worked hard to ingratiate herself, chattering gaily, telling her best stories with all the animation and dramatic flair she could muster, trying to amuse Estela so she would be welcomed back.

But even Estela was not always a willing hostess.

"She didn't even offer me a glass of water," my mother would whisper to me after we left. But she didn't dare tell Papá of these snubs; he might not want to take her into town if he knew.

I felt enormously sad for my mother at these times. It was unfair that she had to perform and humiliate herself just to get a day off the farm.

Her frustration manifested itself in weight gain and increased smoking.

"I'm going crazy on this farm!" she'd rant in desperate moments. "After all these years of living in the middle of nowhere, deprived of human contact, all we have to show for the sacrifice is nothing—not one cent!"

In our early days on the farm when Papá had built her a hutch in the kitchen and a carport outside, she had tried to encourage some entrepreneurial spirit in him.

"With your carpentry skills, you could fix houses. We could buy houses and rent them. People who can do their own repairs do well in real estate," she'd say.

Papá would nod agreeably but not have much to say. My mother was always full of ideas and projects for businesses.

Before they married they had even considered opening a Mexican restaurant with Estela and her husband, Miguel. That project fell through but it didn't stop my mother from coming up with other ventures, including a vegetable stand at the entrance to the farm. Don Ray nixed that one, saying that everything grown on the farm was his, not hers to sell.

My mother's frustration was full of pent-up resentment and anger. She stood in the middle of the kitchen in her flowered house dress, now a middle-aged, heavy-set woman, looking sad and dowdy.

"I don't even know how to drive, speak English, or dial a phone. That's what being trapped on this farm has done for me—made me a good-for-nothing."

Her lower lip trembled, tears sprang from her eyes and slid down her cheeks.

"The farm deprived you too, *mi'ja,*" she said to me. "You could have taken dance lessons, piano lessons, and learned to swim. I wanted all those things for you. Instead you have this: a solitary life."

The money arguments between my parents increased too. How could they ever move into town and buy their own house if my father never saved? my mother demanded. She tried reasoning with him about the need for budgets and planning, but he resented her, interpreting her words as criticism. He avoided money discussions, bought whatever he wanted—expensive movie cameras, projectors, automotive tools—and dismissed her concerns with the words *"Estás loca."*

<hr />

IN SECOND GRADE, A REPRESENTATIVE from the Bank of America came to our class and encouraged us to save, even if it meant depositing only a few pennies a week. "Pennies grow to dollars," he said.

Every week I brought my bankbook home and my parents gave me money to deposit. Our teacher collected the books in a canvas bag every Friday, to be returned the following week. It thrilled me to see the new date and deposit neatly stamped on the page. And the balance was growing. I believed what the man from the bank promised—that if we conscientiously saved every week, we'd have enough money to buy a car when we turned eighteen.

What I didn't understand was that the savings was really my parents' money and not mine exclusively. Over the years, with unexpected medical emergencies, car repairs, taxes, needy relatives, and travels to Mexico, the money in the bankbook fluctuated like the weather.

22

HOME IN TOWN

THE NEWS WAS SUDDEN AND UNEXPECTED. Don Ray was giving up the lease to the farm on Jolon Road. He would be farming another spread, which although it did have a house for us to use, was farther away and deeper in the country.

We knew the place; a farmer named Brickey had lived there. It was a well-built farmhouse with a large kitchen, a sun-dappled living room, and a walnut tree that canopied the front yard in the spring and summer. We also knew that when it rained the dirt road that curved its way around the hills and meadows to the blacktop road turned into mud and there'd be no way to get out of the farm.

The idea of further isolation horrified my mother.

"It's too impractical," she told Papá. "How would Rosela get to school? What happens if there's an emergency and we can't get out because the road is gone?"

Don Ray gave us one month to leave the *casa grande*. Both my parents panicked.

"There's not enough time to find a house to buy," my mother lamented. Papá worried how he'd ever be able to pay for one.

Luckily, an answer came in the form of Mrs. Bane, the eccentric old woman we used to visit when we lived in Mrs. Maggie's boarding house. Mrs. Bane was now eighty-five and had decided to move from the corner house to one of her smaller rental units. She offered to rent us the house until we found one to buy. It was not the best of solutions, just the only one available.

Living at Mrs. Bane's pressured Papá more than anything else to actively search for a house to buy. Mrs. Bane was senile and meddlesome, constantly complaining about imaginary slights and problems. She had become churlish and mean-spirited in her old age, and she drove both my parents crazy. My mother managed their relationship by limiting her exposure to the old lady.

Papá's weekly visits to the realtor finally paid off. He came in excitedly one night to say they'd found a house he could afford to buy. The realtor told him he could easily take out a bank loan and the monthly payments would be as low as the rent we were paying. Seeing Papá look so pleased lifted our spirits, and we chattered brightly all the way to the house. It was on the opposite side of town, around the corner from the Catholic church. Houses stood on either side of it and in front was a big empty lot. Across from the house on the corner was nothing but empty fields. We walked up a broken cement path that led through a patchy lawn full of weeds and crabgrass. The owners, an older couple, said hello. The wife, a fat, cross-eyed woman who smelled of liquor, followed us around as the realtor showed us the interior. There wasn't much to it—a small living room, a kitchen, two bedrooms with one bathroom between them, and a porch. The house was much smaller than either Mrs. Bane's rental or the house we'd lived in on the farm. The wife seemed sad to be selling it, though. "We're going back to Arkansas," the bald-headed husband told us, even though no one had asked.

"It's on a double lot. Big enough to build another house in the back," the realtor pointed out. My heart sank. I thought it had to be the ugliest house in King City. I looked at my mother. I couldn't read her expression but there was a shadow in her eyes. But Papá was sold on it—or perhaps just the price. My mother asked about another house she and Papá had seen. She liked it better but it was more expensive.

That night I heard her say, "I know it's a bigger debt, but now that we're in town, I'll be able to work. I'll help you pay for it."

"We have to buy what we can afford right now. What if you can't find work? Then we'd lose the house."

My mother reluctantly agreed with Papá.

"What do you think? Do you really like the house?" she asked me.

"I don't know. I guess. I mean, do *you* like it?" My answer was deliberately vague. I suspected my mother didn't like the house and was looking for reinforcement from me. If I said I hated the house, it would give her the courage to tell Papá she didn't like it. But then he'd get mad at me for messing up his perfect real estate deal. I just wanted them to make their own decision. I figured they'd be the ones living there for a long time, not me. I planned to go to college and leave King City. I hadn't shared that with my mother yet, though. I still had a few years of school and figured senior year would be soon enough to tell her.

"I think we'll buy it," my mother announced with a sigh. "It does have that large backyard. Eventually we can add on, maybe build a bigger kitchen and another bathroom. Your father is a talented carpenter. If he wanted, he could make this place something."

I wanted to say, "When has he ever made anything something?" but bit my tongue. My mother had made a disappointing decision and was trying to make it positive. I knew I would hate living there.

The first thing we did when we moved in was paint everything yellow. It was my mother's favorite color and she said it cheered up any house. Papa mixed the wrong shade for the living room and wound up with a bright canary yellow. It looked like the inside of a cheap motel, but we didn't say anything. He was irritable from painting all day and dangerously close to losing his temper. If he did, he'd stop talking to us and not paint the rest of the house. "It's beautiful," my mother forced herself to say.

There were many projects to complete inside the house, but instead Papá inexplicably took it upon himself that first weekend to break up the cement sidewalk with a jackhammer. He banged and banged on it all morning until my mother marched out and demanded, "Why are you doing that?"

"I'm taking out the sidewalk and then I'll pour new cement to make a smooth walkway."

"That sounds great, but I need you in here to help me with things in the kitchen and bathroom or else I won't be able to cook and you won't be able to bathe."

Papá glared at her, threw the hammer down, and walked away. The older he got the shorter his fuse. Mamá said his diabetes made him cranky. He returned a few hours later, cooled off and ready to help my mother. He never finished the walkway, leaving it uglier than it was before he took a jackhammer to it.

The other projects he tackled had similar results. Papá's carpentry skills seemed not what my mother remembered.

My mother found work that first summer in the tomato packing shed sorting tomatoes on the conveyor belt. She stayed employed from then on.

23

EDITH WINSLOW

IT BECAME CLEAR TO ME IN HIGH SCHOOL that I had limited professional possibilities.

My parents had no college ambitions for me, but then again neither did my teachers or counselors. To them, graduating from high school was a sufficiently commendable accomplishment. My parents' limited aspirations, however, didn't mean they didn't care about education. It just wasn't within their realm of possibilities. In Mexico, girls had small careers or jobs until they married.

My mother offered a choice of role models from her world perspective.

"You can be a bilingual secretary like your cousin Silvia. You already know English; you just have to learn shorthand and typing. Or you can work at the Bank of America, like Miss García. I'm sure they'd hire another Mexican girl, especially someone as smart as you."

It's not that I didn't think her suggestions were worthy of my consideration. The truth of the matter was that I was afraid to tell my mother I was a fraud. I couldn't get the hang of shorthand and dropped the class because I was on the verge of a D. My typing was slow at best and my eyes crossed at the thought of taking a bookkeeping class.

My vocational skills were also limited. I got fired for mixing up orders at the restaurant I worked at for a few weeks. After filling in for another employee at a retail store and being told I would likely keep the job after she returned, I was not invited to stay. It seems I was too slow at making change, which made for long waits and impatient customers.

Even my domestic abilities were lacking. I was hopeless at making tortillas; my dough turned out mushy or hard. When I tried to make smooth balls and pat them into nice round circles like my mother, they came out in weird oblong shapes. My hands frequently had burn marks from turning over the tortillas on the *comal*. I never mastered the gist of softening corn husks for tamales (I let them get too soggy), nor did I learn how to tear the straight corn husk strips used to tie the tamales together. There was either too much filling or not enough and, inevitably, a big gooey mess. I hated the interminable canning process I had to go through every summer and I found ways to avoid helping my mother. And to add insult to injury, I must have been the only girl in the history of home economics in my school to get a C for the semester—all because I couldn't sew a straight hem or cook some stupid main dish.

Because of these shortcomings I immersed myself in a whirlwind of extracurricular activities. I was in the speech and debate club, the thespian club, and on the yearbook and newspaper staffs. It was both a way of exploring my latent talents as well as a way of belonging at school, which was far more important at the time.

I knew I was good in one thing and that was writing. I had entertained myself writing stories since grade school. It finally paid off in eighth grade, when Mrs. Phillips declared me the best writer in my class. At my eighth-grade graduation she presented me with a writing award and gave me the only A in English class. My schoolmates accepted her pronouncement without question and during a graduation skit two "gypsies" looked into a crystal ball and saw that I was destined to be a writer.

Unfortunately, writing had little currency in my world.

"*Ay, mi'ja.* Writing stories is not a job or career. You can't earn a salary to support yourself," my mother lamented.

I must have shared this conversation with my former eighth-grade teacher because she insisted I go meet with her friend Edith Winslow to talk about a profession I had never heard about called "journalism."

On the phone Edith Winslow sounded curt and hurried. She agreed to meet with me at the offices of the *Rustler Herald* newspaper, where she was the only female reporter on staff, she made sure to tell me. My mother found out she was the society page editor, the one who wrote about weddings and social gatherings. Even the Mexican ladies knew about her because she liked to practice her heavily accented, broken Spanish with them, in the process encouraging them to submit their birth and wedding announcements, which she actually published, something unheard of before she arrived. For this and other displays of individual spirit, some people described her as eccentric.

I wasn't quite sure what to expect when I showed up at the offices of the *Rustler Herald*. Edith appeared from behind a glass door. She was a tall, lanky red-haired woman with large black-rimmed glasses wearing a stylish blue two-piece knit suit and black high heels. She walked briskly and extended her hand, grasping mine tightly and shaking it vigorously.

"I'm Edith Winslow."

"Nice to meet you, Mrs. Winslow..."

"No. I'm not Mrs. Winslow, I'm Edith."

She was unlike anyone I had ever met. Her brusque, forthright manner was both intimidating and appealing.

"So, you want to talk journalism?" she said from behind a wooden desk piled with papers.

"I don't really know much about...that is, I don't know what journalism is about," I stammered.

"It's what I do. This is a newspaper. We report the news. The news is what's going on this town, the state, or the world. It can be a fire, an accident, or what's decided in a city council meeting. I go out and get the facts, get the information, and I come back and write it into a story. It appears here," she said dramatically, sweeping her hand over the pile of newspapers on one corner of her desk.

"And you get paid, like a job?" I asked nervously.

"It's more than a job. Journalism is a mission. Journalists are seekers of truth, stewards of—" Edith stopped her passionate speech. She cocked her head at me, gave me a funny look, and practically barked, "Damn right I get paid. I may be the only woman on this newspaper, but I don't do it for charity. I work as hard as any man and I'm just as good. Maybe even better!"

"Well, the only thing I'm any good at is writing. Everybody tells me I won't be able to get a job so I should be a secretary or clerk instead."

"What a bunch of baloney! Who told you this? That's one of the things I hate about this place—these provincial minds!" Edith said, angrily rising from her seat.

I was only fifteen years old and Edith was probably well into her forties, but I felt an immediate bond, a psychic connection that let me know this was a kindred spirit.

"You think you might want to be a journalist?"

"I think so," I nodded happily.

"Are you willing to work hard? Becoming a journalist won't be easy," she warned.

"I'll work very hard if writing is part of my job."

"Then I'll help you," she said solemnly.

I had learned that adults had a habit of saying things just to be nice, never having any intention of following through. But in time I would realize that Edith never ever said anything she didn't mean. She made a commitment to be my mentor that day and she never wavered.

I stood by my commitment, too. Freshmen were not allowed to join the high school newspaper staff, but I petitioned to get in and did. I made a name for myself second semester by writing a scathing editorial attacking a new testing schedule. Two seniors congratulated me and told me my editorial had made a great impact. They said my article made teachers and administrators question their decision and take the issue to the student council. I was amazed that my words could influence events! It was my first glimpse into the power of journalism.

My high school days were further enhanced by Edith Winslow's sponsorship. She took it upon herself to promote every single victory I accomplished in school by featuring me in articles and photographs in the weekly town paper. There I'd be on the front page of the *Rustler Herald* grinning, holding a huge trophy for winning a Lion's Club speech contest. Then as first runner-up for the Junior Miss pageant. Later a photo of me with other student leaders. And endless articles and pictures of me at innumerable speech contests and student activities.

She must have sensed my feelings of alienation and insecurity, and I believe the constant publicity was her way of bolstering my self-confidence. But she also provided meaningful experiences that served to develop my skills as a writer and journalist. Edith was instrumental in my selection as the high school columnist for the *Rustler Herald*. Later, with her help, I cinched a newspaper internship as well as a college scholarship.

I was invited to her house for dinner only once. She lived in a tony cul-de-sac in what was considered the upper-crust part of town. Her home was a contemporary ranch whose front door was adorned by a peace sign. She was against the Vietnam War and had no compunctions about expressing her liberal views in this conservative farming community. Her husband was the town optometrist and they had no children, just a Siamese cat.

I thought her house quite sophisticated, from the sectional sofa set to the abstract art and Indian pottery in the living room.

She served red wine with dinner. "In Europe even children drink wine. Have you ever had wine?"

"Oh, sure," I lied.

She smiled knowingly but said nothing.

Everything about that evening seemed terribly glamorous to me. They regaled me with stories about their travels, including trips to Mexico. They often stayed in San Francisco to attend the theater and were still talking about how much she loved the popular musical *Hair*. I had asked her to write a review of it for the school newspaper some time before and she had done so with gusto.

The review started with typical Edith exuberance: "Would you write a review of *Hair* for us?" asked a KCHS reporter. She could easily have asked "Would you put your head in a lion's mouth?"

Three single-spaced columns later it ended: "*Hair* is interesting, it is NOW, it is intriguing. It is NOT a good show."

Sometime during the evening the conversation took an unexpected turn. Edith's husband, who had been drinking more than us, suddenly blurted out, "I don't know, Edith. I just don't think you should be encouraging her to be a journalist so much. She has no contacts or family connections. And then being Mexican. You know what it takes."

Edith's face turned as red as her hair. "Really, Bob. Everybody has a chance."

He slumped in his chair, his face puffy, his glasses tipped almost to the end of his nose, making him look silly and old. He crossed his arms and proceeded to stare at the floor. I felt confused. Part of me knew that he had meant well, but in my experiences with well-meaning people, I had discovered that their words and actions were often no less hurtful than someone who acted with deliberation.

That night I had an epiphany. I decided I no longer wanted to be understanding. I resented Bob's negative words. I even allowed that I didn't think much of Bob. I vowed I would not let anyone stand in the way of my chosen career path. I would do it to prove him wrong and I would do it to prove her right.

24

DRAGGING MAIN

LIKE SO MANY ADOLESCENTS, my teenage years were a time of alienation from my parents, their world, and the small town where we lived. One of my chief escapes was dragging Main with my friends. But other than cars going up and down the street, my experience bears little resemblance to George Lucas's *American Graffiti*. I recall one night vividly.

A car honks insistently outside the house. Karen and Erline are here. I look through my bedroom door into the living room and see my mother shake her head. She exchanges looks with my father.

Honk! Honk!

"In Mexico only taxis honk for people to leave their house. *Gente decente* come to the door, greet the family, maybe even enjoy a refreshment before going for a ride." My mother had always divided the world into two groups: *gente decente*, "nice Mexicans," and some gringos, and then all others—low-class Mexicans, Okies, and the rest of the gringos. My friends didn't count because they were still teenagers.

I impatiently brush my long black hair, trying to make it as straight as Cher's. My arm aches from the effort and I put the brush down, watching my hair spring back into its natural wave.

"Ugh!" I sigh.

Karen and Erline are so lucky with their long, straight, blonde hair.

I run to the window and gesture with my hand for them to wait. The two light heads bob simultaneously. From a distance they look identical. It's only close up that you see long-faced Karen is tall and slender and Erline is short and round. Their personalities are also different. Karen is sweet-natured and quiet while Erline can be sharp-tongued and sarcastic. She makes us laugh until our sides ache. Lately, though, I've begun to feel that Karen and Erline are more alike than different. That I'm the oddball. It's not just my coloring either, it's little things. Things I can't put my finger on.

Now I see Karen laugh as she pantomimes honking the horn again. I notice they're both wearing pastel Western shirts. I'm wearing a striped knit top with bellbottom jeans. Shoot! There's no time to change. What am I saying? I don't even own a Western shirt! I sling my embroidered yellow Indian bag over my shoulder and cross into the living room.

Papá grunts. He reaches for a bowl of walnuts on the low imitation-wood coffee table without taking his eyes off the fast-talking, Spanish-speaking newscasters on the TV screen. He and I have little to say to each other these days. My mother says Mexican fathers believe girls are a mother's responsibility. I can't decide what irritates me more, his conversation or his silence. One thing I am certain of—I don't want to stay too often in the house.

Sighing audibly, my mother sinks into the orange and brown flowered sofa, tucking her feet under her. She's worked nine hours sorting garlic on a conveyor belt. I feel a surge of sympathy seeing her huddled on the couch. She pulls a cigarette out of her pack of Trues and tells me not to be home too late.

"*Sí,* Mamá," I murmur. I see her face relax as she blows a wisp of smoke. "I never inhale," she often states, justifying her pack-a-day habit.

I kiss her lightly on the cheek, breathing in her scent of garlic and tobacco, and then hurriedly step over my father's outstretched feet, muttering *"Adiós."* He burps in response.

Sugar, pa-pa-pa-pa-pa-pa,
Aah, honey, honey, pa-pa-pa-pa-pa-pa,
You are my candy girl,
And you got me wanting you.

The Archies blare from Karen's mother's navy blue Mercury.
I slide across the front seat next to Erline, who grins, saying,
"Let's get truckin', girls!" I've crossed the border from obedient
Mexican daughter to liberated American teenager.

"Karen Sue and I did a little scouting down Main already. Not
too many guys yet," Erline says, brushing her hair. Her gleaming
gold locks, the color of wheat in the autumn sun, shimmer with
each vigorous stroke.

"Any cute guys at all?" I ask.

"All the cute guys are gone—they're in college or 'Nam,"
Erline answers dryly.

What we have in common is that we're all wallflowers. We
don't go to school dances because we're never asked to dance,
and only Karen has been to a formal. The guy who took her
died in Vietnam a year later.

"Can you believe we're seniors?" Karen says in her whispery
little-girl voice.

"Seniors and still no boyfriends!" Erline retorts. "I'll tell you
guys one thing for sure: I'm gonna have a date before I graduate.
I'm not graduating a wallflower. Goddam, if I do, I just know I'll
end up an old maid in this shitty town."

Karen giggles. She punches the car radio buttons until she
finds The Archies again. "Don't you just love that song?"

Erline elbows Karen, who pushes her back, squealing, "Quit
it!" Erline starts giggling and pretty soon they're both laughing
hysterically and jabbing each other. I force a tight smile. They
can be so immature.

I glance out the window as we pass Vanderhurst Street.
Mulberry trees line both sides of the road, looking like bogey-
men slouched in the dark. Flickers of light from TV sets glare
out of the houses that sit back from the street. No lights illumi-
nate the wide road, nothing moves. It's 8:00 p.m. and everyone
appears to be settled in for the night.

As we turn onto Broadway our eyes blink as they adjust to
the bright lights. Every storefront is lit up like a Vegas marquee.

Our tires squeak as we turn to fall in line with the cars that are already cruising up and down the ten-block length. I roll down the car window and Erline turns up the volume on the radio until it makes me wince. Karen is driving slowly and we can hear the blaring of other car radios on the street.

Once, U.S. 101 passed right through Broadway. Cars with out-of-state license plates formed a lively caravan. Just knowing that the people inside were heading for destinations beyond this town made them seem glamorous to me. Now the people with places to go and stories to tell fill their tanks at gas stations off the freeway exits and only occasionally wander into town to eat at Keefer's Restaurant. Otherwise, the only traffic is on Friday and Saturday nights when high schoolers take over to drag Main Street.

We sit thigh to thigh and pass Dick Bruhner's (cute boys work there), Hitchcock's Pharmacy (where my mother picks up all her prescriptions), Becky's Western Wear (I spent all my summer earnings there last summer), Tri's Supermarket (where my mother embarrassed me by selling rabbits for extra income), the Reel Joy Theater (I'll never forget seeing "A Hard Day's Night" there, where now only Mexican movies are shown), the JC Penney catalog store (everybody knows that if you buy clothes there everyone will wind up wearing the same thing), and the El Camino Real Hotel (the place we arrived at when we came from Mexico).

We hang a U-turn where the street ends at the railroad tracks next to the Brown's Vegetable Packing Shed, where my mom and I worked one summer. The radio starts playing "Incense and Peppermints" and Karen pushes the buttons until she finds The Archies again. I start to protest but Erline has already begun to hum. I hate "bubblegum" music as much as Erline and Karen seem to love it.

There are no people on the streets except those in front of saloons. Young Mexican farmworkers. They whistle low and appreciatively at every woman who drives by. Karen shudders

and Erline grimaces. In Mexico *piropos* are meant to be flirta-
tious, vaguely complimentary, but Americans always react with
disgust. I don't even consider explaining this to my friends.
Instead I act grossed out, too.

Erline and Karen are practically the only girls from school
who ever come over to my house. I hate our house. Papá found
some surplus green paint on sale, and now the house looks like a
nopal. A brown vinyl couch sitting forlornly on the front porch is
another of Papá's home improvement projects. He decided to
learn upholstery from instructions on a vinyl kit, and it turned
out a big mess. Now Mamá's six cats use it as a scratching post.
Mamá is always nagging him to take it to the dump. He's been
saying he will for so long, but that junky couch has become a
fixture. Another reason not to talk to Papá.

Erline has never invited me to her house. She says she lives
too far out of town. I know she lives in a trailer with her parents, who look like her grandparents; she's one of those change-
of-life babies. Papá says he knows the farm where her father
works as a ranch hand. It's outside San Lucas, almost at the foot
of the mountains. If she's embarrassed about her trailer house, I
know what she feels like.

I guess that's why we always wind up at Karen's. It's a neat,
clean ranch-style filled with maple furniture, the kind of house
I've seen in magazines and would like for myself someday.

"There's Jake Thompson." Karen points to a rusted green
pickup truck. Inside a long-faced boy wearing a stained cowboy
hat looks away, pretending he doesn't know us. Two fat farm
boys snicker next to him. Jake and one of the fat boys are in my
speech class. Everyone rolls their eyes, listening to them stumble
reading two-syllable words. I think they're stupid, but Karen and
Erline find them cute.

"Oh, God! There's Marcia riding with Zev Roberts," Erline
gasps. Marcia is the head pom-pom girl. Zev's going to some
school back east where he's studying pre-med. His father is a big
shot in town.

Zev Roberts and I had journalism together my freshman year, and I liked him immediately. We were the only two in class who were interested in talking about things like the civil rights movement and free speech. He is smart and clever, and the first person to introduce me to reading columnist Herb Caen in the *San Francisco Chronicle*.

"You still moony about that guy?" Erline asks, shaking her head. "You know guys like Zev don't date no Mexicans, or Okie gals, for that matter," she elbows Karen, who snorts obligingly.

That Okie accent always surfaces when she refers to Karen and herself or her family. I find it degrading. It is akin to my using a Mexican accent to talk about myself.

"I've sent out my college applications. You guys all done?" I change the subject.

"Nope. Haven't sent any."

"Me neither," Karen chimes in.

"I thought you guys were going to JC in Salinas?"

"Oh, probably," Erline shrugs. "There's still time for that. I can't think of anything to major in and I can't stand the idea of more school."

"Me neither," Karen nods.

"But if you don't go to school, what will you do? The only jobs in town are clerking at the Bank or Basic."

"Hey, we're not intellectuals like you. You know what you want to do. Karen Sue and I, we just don't have any burning passion to study one thing or another."

"Maybe we'll just get lucky and get married," Karen giggles.

They both laugh. I don't find this funny at all but smile dully at them. The car feels like it's closing in on me. I open the window and breathe in a mixture of exhaust fumes and garlic.

"Well, looky there! I do declare," Erline sings out.

"Whatcha lookin' at?" Karen's blonde hair whips around her face as she jerks her head from side to side, trying to look at both sides of the street.

"There! On the corner of Foster's Freeze. Look at those dudes!"

Karen swerves the car as she cranes her neck to look. We scream, bumping into each other.

"Go around again!" Erline yells.

We loop around Broadway. It's 9:00 p.m. and more cars have joined the impromptu Saturday night parade of teenage drivers. There are more familiar faces, some friendly, others that look right through us. We no longer care about any of them; Erline has spotted some interesting guys. Maybe football players from Gonzales High School, our arch rival, or maybe FFAers (Future Farmers of America club members) from Soledad High. My friend Judy and I had once met some real cute guys at the King City Fair when we were freshman. We had walked around with them but then her mother showed up out of the blue and gave us no opportunity to exchange phone numbers.

"Hija," my mother had admonished me when she found out. "Nice girls don't go around walking with strange boys. You don't know their families."

Judy had fared worse with her mother, who scolded her in front of me. "Is that what you want to be—a floozy? Because that's just how you're acting, missy. Like a cheap floozy, an easy pickup!"

Karen slows down in front of the Foster's Freeze drive-in. Oh, no, I think, disappointed. It's just a group of "doggies," soldiers from Fort Hunter Liggett, standing around grinning and waving.

"Over here, girls," one of them calls out.

"Let's go talk to them." Erline shoves me out the door.

My heart sinks. Three skinny guys with shorn heads approach us enthusiastically. My eyes are drawn instantly to their heavy black military shoes, short-sleeved, short-waisted, pastel-print shirts, and navy blue bellbottoms that are real sailor pants, not the kind that are in style. I swallow my disgust. Erline and Karen are actually smiling.

"Hey, what's your name?" one says, looking directly at Erline.

"You tell me first," she says, flirting.

Donny, Harvey, and Tom introduce themselves. Harvey goes and stands next to Erline. Donny stares openly at Karen. That leaves Tom. He doesn't make a move toward me or try to lock eyes with me as Donny is doing with Karen.

"So, where you from, soldier?" I ask.

"West Virginia." His accent sounds funny and Southern.

"What did you do there?"

"Joined the Army."

"Did you go to high school or were you in college?

"Yep. Two years."

"You're a college sophomore?" I say, surprised.

Tom guffaws. "Shoot, no. Two years high school."

"Oh." I'm disappointed. He was just beginning to seem kind of good-looking. "Why didn't you finish?"

Tom shrugs. He looks bored. "Had to get married."

I begin to feel as if my clothes are too tight. I can't breathe. I have to move. I walk over to the picnic tables where the others have sat down and are talking and laughing. Tom follows me.

"Hey, guys, I really have to get home," I say as lightly and apologetically as I can.

"You just got here," Harvey grins. Erline and Karen glare at me. Harvey actually seems nice. His eyes are soft and sympathetic like a kind older brother's. When he speaks, his accent is Southern too, but smoother, not as gruff as Tom's. Curious, I ask if they all come from the same town. This sets them all chortling at once.

"Heck, no. Tom's from West Virginia, Donny's a mountain boy from the Ozarks, and me, I hail from Tennessee." Harvey playfully pokes round-faced Donny, whose hair is so blonde he almost looks like an albino. Donny and Tom don't say much. Harvey's the talker and he directs all the conversation to Erline. Donny stares at Karen with a gap-toothed smile on his face.

I sit with my back turned to the traffic, praying no one sees me hanging out with doggies. Everyone knows only desperate girls go out with doggies. That's what ruined Linda Sue's reputation. They say she'll sleep with any soldier who can buy her drugs. I still say "hi" to her even though no one else will. I don't care who sees me—I can't be mean to the first girl that befriended me in town.

"What do you girls do for fun?" Donny leers at Karen.

"Go out drinkin' beer," Erline says, a wild look in her eyes.

I roll my eyes. Who is she kidding? I can't believe she said that!

"You girls seem, um, a little young for that," Harvey smiles in his brotherly way. "How about driving around with us?"

A newspaper headline flashes across my mind: "Missing! Three High School Girls!"

We don't know anything about these guys. It's not like hanging out with the boys at school we've known since first grade. These soldiers are strangers, outsiders. My mother's always pointing out some story in the *Salinas Californian* about soldiers from Fort Ord committing one crime or another.

"I'm sorry, Karen. I have to go home now or my mom will kill me."

Karen and Erline exchange looks. The boys' bodies tense.

"You go ahead and take her home. I'll wait for you back here," Erline waves her hand dismissively at me. Her face is bland, expressionless, but her eyes are intense. It's as if she's become another person. I don't know her anymore.

Karen jumps up good-naturedly and smiles slyly at Donny. "See you," she giggles. Donny blushes; it makes him look sick.

The familiar smells of Karen's car reassure me and I sink into the seat.

"Do you really like those guys?" I ask tentatively.

"It's just for fun," Karen says a little too defensively.

"But they're soldiers." I emphasize "soldiers," trying to convey my disapproval.

"It's not like we're going to marry them or anything," she laughs.

Reaching over to the radio she punches buttons until she finds The Archies.

Sugar, pa-pa-pa-pa-pa-pa,
Aah, honey, honey, pa-pa-pa-pa-pa-pa,

You are my candy girl,
And you got me wanting you.

After she drops me off, I stand there as the car lights and
music slowly fade and the dark street swallows the car. Mamá has
left the porch light on. It outlines the torn Naugahyde couch
and cracked cement steps leading to the front door. A quarter
moon hangs like an ornament in a black starless sky. Crickets
chirp softly. I plop myself down on the lawn, leaning on my
hands behind my back on the overgrown grass that needs mow-
ing. I smell the fragrance of sweet Mexican jasmine my mother
smuggled in to plant in our front yard. A slight breeze stirs and
blows a shiver underneath my blouse. I hug my knees to my
chest, not wanting to go inside the house. I'm not sorry I didn't
stay with my friends. For the moment, here, outside, is the only
place I belong.

25

THE SHADOW OF CÉSAR CHÁVEZ

IT WAS 1970 AND EVERYBODY WAS TALKING about César Chávez. The farmers in our area were tense because he'd moved the UFW headquarters from Delano to Salinas.

By the late sixties the bracero program that provided cheap laborers for the growers was over. In its place migrant workers and seasonal labor toiled in the fields, orchards, and packing sheds. They worked for low wages, without benefits or health insurance. They were prime recruits for the United Farm Workers union, but the growers had cut a deal with the Teamsters union to undercut the UFW's efforts. The Teamsters signed contracts with major lettuce growers and began recruiting field workers. Chávez's move to Salinas was not only strategic but critical to the union's survival.

The emergence of the scarlet flags with the black eagle waving over fields created as much controversy among the agricultural workers as it did among the growers. There was no unanimity among the Mexican laborers. Some believed in the more powerful Teamsters union, some in the UFW. Others didn't have faith in any union. Many were simply afraid. They feared losing jobs they depended on to raise large families. Migrants who came year after year like the seasons didn't want to be blackballed by growers who held jobs for them. They didn't have the luxury to support a fledgling union. Confusion, rumors, and tension swirled like a harvester blade through the bucolic landscape of the Salinas Valley.

My family reflected those ambivalences.

"Do you think the Chavistas will come to your *rancho*?" my mother asked my father.

He shrugged. "Won't do any good. Won't get any recruits there."

"You don't think any of the men will join the union?"

"Only the lazy ones who'd rather parade around carrying flags than work."

Papá was very clear about where he stood. He didn't believe a farmworkers union could ever match the strength of the Teamsters, a union deeply entrenched in the valley. He didn't believe Mexicans—poor, uneducated Mexicans like himself— could hang together long enough to succeed.

"There's always *envidias* that get in the way. *Por eso no progresamos.* That's why we don't progress," he'd argue.

I wondered if Papá saw himself as having progressed. He was a man who had taught himself phonetic English from a tattered English/Spanish dictionary. He wrote those English words correctly in elegant script handwriting. He could put together and take apart car engines from reading a manual. But I never saw anyone outside our family ever express support for him. Americans winced and grew impatient with his heavily accented English, often responding curtly and turning quickly away so as not to encourage further conversation. He was difficult to understand. He didn't articulate properly and he stammered, hemmed and hawed, grasping for the right words. And when words failed, he relied on sounds. I remember one painful exchange with my high school English teacher.

"Schee don-a likee dee numbers. That why schee-a likee dee writing so much. Aha. Schee write zip-zip-zip but de numbers—ha! Oh, boy!"

Of course, that's not how he sounded in Spanish. He was not only articulate, he could be downright eloquent. But over time, I had seen him retreat. He anticipated Americans' response to his speech, his dark skin, and his Indian features. I saw it in the slump of his shoulders, in the downward cast of his eyes, in the downward curve of his mouth.

Perhaps that's why he never had much faith in men like himself fighting the external world on his behalf. Perhaps his imagination couldn't conjure images of respect and success among brown-skinned men with cracked, dry hands and dust-rimmed eyes.

My mother stayed neutral. She listened to my father and asked questions without expressing an opinion.

"What do you think of Chávez, Mamá?" I asked.

"*Pobrecito.* He has such a struggle. That little man against those big, rich farmers." She shook her head sympathetically. "Farmworkers suffer so much. They need someone to help them."

I had not yet had a political awakening, and I, not unlike my mother, reacted to issues viscerally. Vietnam was about losing some of our older classmates, boys some of my girlfriends had dated. Our senior class debated over building a memorial to those boys, and a handful of classmates who considered themselves antiwar campaigned against the memorial. They wore their hair long, defied the dress code by wearing American flags on their shirts, and generally annoyed school administrators by constantly protesting everything from school codes to the campus sprinkler system. Most of the students reflected their parents' conservative leanings or were plainly apolitical. Members of the Future Farmers of America—the biggest club on campus—resented hippies and proudly displayed "America: Love It or Leave It" bumper stickers on their rusted pickup trucks. When my speech class debated whether or not to legalize marijuana, I took the "con" side and handily defeated the proponent—and this judged by a jury of peers.

The school newspaper was a record of our interests. In its pages we declared the miniskirt dead and the maxi "in." One student reporter wrote about a concert by the group It's a Beautiful Day that he had traveled all the way to Salinas to attend. Most of the stories were about overachieving students:

Student of the Week, Junior Miss contestants, Boys and Girls State delegates. All this when I was the newspaper editor.

Nobody at school talked about farmworkers, César Chávez, or the union. The MAYA Club (Mexican American Youth Association), the only Mexican American group on campus, focused their energy on choosing a Cinco de Mayo Queen.

Yet, it was not all business as usual. A sense of danger and tension lurked at the back doors, in the parking lots and alleyways of the small town, and on anonymous fields and remote farms in the area. It was as palpable in the grocery stores where the workers shopped alongside growers' wives as it was in the church pews where they worshipped together yet separately.

One day I received a phone call from the wife of one of the more prominent growers. She wanted me to translate into Spanish something that was to be published in the local paper. It was the growers' response to an open letter Chávez had written to Salinas Valley workers. Upset that the paper had stooped to even print the "rabble-rouser's demands," the growers had decided it was to their benefit to write their side. That way they could use the printed material to make flyers and distribute them to all of the farmworkers.

I was flattered to have such an important caller seek me out, project such trust and confidence in my abilities, and treat me as an "insider." I quickly accepted her offer, and the second I hung up the phone I ran to tell my mother.

"They come to you—a young girl—for help?"

Her response was a little irritating. She knew I was the high school correspondent for the paper. And probably the only Mexican American in town who knew anything about journalism. It was obvious to me they would naturally think of me! I would have checked with Edith, who might know more about this, but she was off on vacation.

I drove down to the newspaper office where the document was being prepared. The grower's wife was as crisp in her manner as the white starched cotton shirt she wore.

"Well, here it is. I'll need it in three days."

"Three days?" I almost choked.

"That's the newspaper deadline, not mine." She paused, placed her glasses on her thin nose, and peered sharply at me. "You *do* know how to write Spanish?"

"Ye-ye-yes, fluently," I stammered.

She smiled encouragingly. "You'll see, it'll go just fine."

She strode purposefully over to the desk as I stood reading the single-spaced copy in tiny print.

"Yes, sir, we'll get that Chávez with this. He doesn't know just who he's dealing with." She punched the air to make her point.

I suddenly felt dizzy. What had I gotten myself into? Her actions made me feel uneasy, but even more troubling was that I had lied about my abilities. I had no formal Spanish language education and was barely literate in written Spanish. In fact, I had only taught myself to read and write with my cousin's first-grade primer, sounding out words carefully and occasionally looking them up in my father's dictionary.

As the woman's voice droned on and on, the only sound I heard was the throbbing of blood vessels pounding in my head. To admit I couldn't translate was to lose face. I reasoned I'd get through it somehow.

"What should I do, Mamá? I don't think I can translate this; it's too complicated," I lamented to my mother when I got home.

"Do you really want to translate this letter?" she asked.

"I already said I would do it. I don't have a choice," I said, exasperated. My mother was being no help at all.

I made an attempt at the first paragraph and realized Papá's battered English/Spanish dictionary would provide no miracles for me.

That's when I came up with a brilliant solution. Of course! I'd ask the Spanish teacher who lived down the block to help me translate.

I ran down the street to Mrs. H's house. She was one of the high school's two Spanish teachers. Mrs. H and her family had escaped from the Castro regime in Cuba, where she and her husband had been prosperous lawyers. They arrived penniless in Chicago, where they had friends or relatives, but unfortunately the bitter Midwest winter and even harsher life as immigrants weakened her husband. He died and she was left to care for her three children. After many struggles she finally landed this job as a Spanish teacher and was happy to have it. (I knew her story because I had interviewed her for the school newspaper under a self-created column I titled "People of Interest.")

I saw Mrs. H look through her peephole before opening the door. I breathlessly explained the situation, emphasizing how much I needed her help.

"Oh, no! I couldn't possibly get involved!" she said, backing away from the doorway.

Astounded, I asked why.

"This is very controversial. It's too political."

Her sad brown eyes glittered with fear. Political? I didn't get it. We weren't in Cuba, for god's sake!

"I'm sorry, I can't help you." She closed the front door and left me standing dumbfounded on her front stoop.

My mother was empathetic. "Ay, poor woman. She comes from a place where politics are a matter of life and death."

"But not here!" I protested.

My mother raised an eyebrow at me meaningfully. I blushed, remembering recent newspaper accounts of bloody confrontations between *huelguistas* and Teamsters.

I worked on the translation feverishly, hunched over Papá's dictionary. I wound up recruiting him to make sure that what I translated made sense. My mother was of no help since she spoke no English. Papá and I worked mostly in silence, occasionally interrupted by his chuckle or guffaw when he read a particularly egregious grammatical error.

When we finally finished, I ventured to ask him, "Do you think it's understandable?"

"Some of it," he said, unable to suppress a laugh.

Then he turned thoughtful as he sat back in his chair. "It's stupid what those growers are saying, anyway. It's lies."

"Well, so maybe it doesn't matter that the translation is messed up," I sighed.

When I delivered my assignment to the grower's wife, I felt I'd aged a year and was no longer impressed by her.

"Please don't use my name as the translator in the paper," I said a little tentatively.

If she was surprised, she didn't show it. She was too engrossed with her mission to squash that "little man."

"Thank you for your help. You've done a great public service for your people."

Her words rang hollow, but my mother's hit their mark.

"She didn't even pay you for all the work you did?" my mother demanded.

I was too embarrassed to admit that it hadn't even occurred to me to negotiate a fee. I had been too caught up in being recognized by one of the town's elite.

"Come on, take me to the grocery store," my mother changed the subject.

In front of the Safeway store stood a cluster of people waving the red and black UFW flags.

"What are you protesting?" I asked.

The young Mexican man told us they were boycotting the lettuce growers and stores that were carrying their lettuce. He asked politely that we support the union by not crossing the picket line.

I looked at my mother, glanced at the store, and watched others pass by and walk in. It occurred to me that this handful of demonstrators was not being terribly persuasive. I started to take a step toward the store but then stopped.

"I don't think I can go in there, Mamá. I'm not going to cross the picket line."

"I don't think I can either, *hija*."

We linked arms and walked away.

26

FIRST DATE

I REMEMBER HOLDING MY BREATH to suppress the surge of excitement that bubbled in the pit of my stomach as I tore open the letter with the foreign stamps. A Kodak Instamatic color photo fell out of the thin, translucent airmail envelope. I stared intensely at the fuzzy photo for a long time, trying to decipher the features of a grinning, brown-haired young man standing in front of military barracks wearing a white T-shirt and green camouflage pants.

My mouth twitched into a tentative smile. I laughed out loud, then covered my mouth self-consciously. He was cute!

My mother and her coworker, a Mexican lady married to an American, had become fast friends at the garlic plant where they worked and they were now playing matchmaker with their children. Mrs. A's son was finishing his tour of duty in Vietnam; he needed a pen pal, she said. A nice girl to write to him, someone who could be his friend when he came home in the summer.

My mother had started a none-too-subtle campaign to draft me for the role. I was hesitant. In my mind there were a number of social land mines that made this a dangerous mission. For starters, I had mixed feelings about Vietnam and had been influenced by my classmates' prejudice against soldiers. Since freshman year in high school, I had known all of the boys who were drafted or had signed up to go to Vietnam. They were our classmates' brothers, the senior boys we flirted with as freshman girls. There was John, who I had known since grammar school. He went to the prom with my friend Paula in May, then to Vietnam after graduation in June, and then he was dead. Our small town had already lost its share of young men.

For four years I'd been watching CBS anchorman Walter Cronkite's nightly news stories vividly detailing gruesome battle scenes in living color from the humid jungles of Vietnam. I also saw my generation on TV marching in antiwar demonstrations, being shot at Kent State, and burning draft cards. I didn't know anyone who had escaped to Canada to avoid the draft or burned their draft card, but in the Salinas Valley, like everywhere else, there was a lot of misdirected acting out. Too often, soldiers on leave became the targets for antiwar protestors. They were viewed as living symbols of and human killing machines for the Vietnam War and not afforded the respect and support other veterans enjoyed. It was a time when police officers were "pigs" and soldiers were "doggies." It was a time one could be stigmatized by being involved with anyone associated with the military if they weren't in your family. It was a time filled with the immaturity, raging hormones, and hubris of a nation of young people coming of age. That's how it was in 1970.

But I also had personal compelling reasons that pushed me into taking a chance on such a correspondence. For one thing, I was feeling left out and lonely. Ever since my only two girlfriends had taken up with their GI boyfriends from Fort Hunter Liggett, I seemed to be the only dateless girl in high school. Karen and Erline didn't care what anyone thought about their dating soldiers. After all, they'd point out, their fellows had never been to 'Nam. They invited me to join them and maybe meet my own GI, but it wasn't for me. I had nothing in common with boys from West Virginia coal mining towns whose greatest ambition was to settle down in a town like King City and work the day shift at the Union Carbide plant.

And then there was my mother. She was worried about me. I overheard her tell my Aunt Tere that at my age she had had dozens of boyfriends, but her own daughter, *ni uno!* With me she tried to be more encouraging.

"If we were in Mexico, you'd have lots of *novios*," she'd say.

I had been raised on stories of her youthful romances. She had filled my head with images of big band dances on sultry summer nights, fragrant gardenias adorning soft hair, and surprise serenades at bedroom windows. Everything she described was *"muy romántico."* Of course, everyone was properly chaperoned, and kissing and handholding were reserved for engaged couples. "If you let them hold your hand, the next thing you know they'll be holding your you-know-whats!" My mother was given this advice by her mother and she was now passing it on to me.

I could have shocked her by telling her what American teenagers were into, but the fact of the matter was that, for me, it was all heresay. I had never been on a date and I certainly had never been kissed! For all I knew, the rumors of what some of my classmates did in the back seats of cars and in barns or cornfields could just be titillating fiction.

I found my interest piqued with every story my mother passed on about this boy "Jimmy."

He went to Palma, the Catholic boys' school in Salinas. He played sports and was in student government. He's an only child, like you, she said. He's a good son. He sends his military pay to his mother. He has an office job because "he's so intelligent." Poor boy got drafted right out of high school.

That was how I found myself looking forward to reading crinkly sheets of rice paper that were full of teasing and playfulness until one arrived with the serious message that he would be home in the summer and could we meet then?

In June I graduated from high school, passed my driver's test, and prepared for college. I received two scholarships and a number of awards for my activities in journalism, speech and debate, drama, and student government. I was heady with my own success. Only one more thing would make it a perfect season: a romance.

Jimmy arrived at the high point of the tomato crop season, when long trucks filled with tomatoes traversed the town at all hours, emptying their cargo in packing sheds where conveyor belts hummed all day and into the night.

It was a still afternoon in July when he bounded up the porch steps and, with a big grin that looked just like it did in his picture, announced, "Hi! I'm Jim."

Once inside the house he glanced quickly around the narrow living room until his eyes stopped on my graduation portrait on the wall. It was a formal photograph taken at Cook's photography studio in Salinas. I wore a white off-the-shoulder fake fur stole. My hair, pulled tightly away from my face, had been painfully styled and teased into an upsweep of curls on top of my head by my mother's friend Rosa. This was the photo I'd mailed to him.

He looked from the portrait to me standing in front of him. I was wearing my hair long and straight below my shoulders, dressed in jeans.

"Boy, that sure doesn't look like you. I was worried you really did look like that," he said, pointing to the wall. "You're actually cute."

I blushed, not knowing whether to be insulted or just pleased because he'd said I was "cute." I giggled instead.

"Here," he said, pushing a box into my hands. "I brought you a present."

Inside a thin cardboard box was a plastic Vietnamese doll dressed in a long purple nylon ethnic dress. I thought it was beautiful.

"Thank you," I murmured, suddenly shy.

We stood staring at each other until I motioned for him to sit down. He crossed his ankle over his knee and started jiggling his foot. I noticed he wasn't very tall but had a pleasant face. His short brown hair was wavy and his eyes smiled as he talked.

"So, what's there to do around here? Let's go for a ride and you can show me."

As we drove around town, he exclaimed over and over how much things had changed in four years. He wanted to know the styles of clothes guys were wearing, what bands were popular, and what TV shows everyone watched.

"I feel like I've been gone for twenty years, everything seems so different!"

He sure wasn't exaggerating about that, I thought. He wore a cotton short-sleeved shirt whose hem touched the top of his belt. The style had been popular in the mid-sixties and was still worn by my male cousins in Mexico. Bell-bottomed pants and Levi jeans were in style, but his pants were narrow-legged brown polyester that weren't long enough to hide the tops of his bulky black military shoes. I was torn between enjoying the idea of riding in a car with a boy and being worried that someone I knew would see me with him.

Jimmy called me the next day, just to talk on the phone. "The folks don't want me out of their sight too much yet," he explained. It sounded to me like, just maybe, he'd rather be with me than his family. Even though he hadn't exactly said so, I felt optimistic. The following day he called again. I wasn't feeling well but I told him he could come by to talk. He agreed and I made him my special Swedish heirloom cookies.

He looked restless the moment he came through the door.

"I have a surprise for you. Look, I made you some cookies."

"Great!" he said, taking a bite.

"Oh, God! These are awful. What's in them?"

I couldn't believe my ears. My parents loved my cookies.

"Well, you're the only one who's never liked them," I said defensively.

"Only one with taste," he teased.

I felt insulted and sat stiffly on the couch. If he noticed my coolness he didn't let on. I turned on the TV. We talked a little. Then he abruptly stood up.

"You know what? It's boring sitting around. Let's go out for a drive!"

"I'm really not up for it today."

"Okay. How about going to the beach later this week?"

"Sure," I answered with a shrug. "You really don't like just talking, do you?"

"You're too serious. Don't you like to go out and have fun?" He said it nicely, not as a jab.

Unknowingly he had struck a nerve. For whatever reasons, I had been excluded from the social aspect of being an American teenager. I had not been invited to parties, on dates, or to a homecoming dance. I had channeled all my energy into succeeding in extracurricular activities, but none of them provided that social entrée I'd longed for.

I didn't dare share this with Jimmy. He seemed nice, but I didn't know him well enough to trust him with my insecurities. It was a matter of pride to pretend to be something I wasn't.

My mother, who considered herself a good judge of character, liked Jimmy immediately and trusted me to go out with him alone. Of course, we only went out during the day, without Papá's knowledge. Maybe my mother had her own agenda for this relationship. After all, I was the one who wanted to go away to college, when she wanted me to stay home and go to Hartnell College in Salinas.

I told my mother I wasn't sure I really liked Jimmy. He teased a lot, we didn't have activities in common, and he didn't want to talk about serious things, like going to college.

"He said he just wants to have fun," I told my mother with disdain.

"You should be more understanding. Think of where he's been, of what he's seen. It's hard to be a schoolboy one day and a soldier the next. He needs time."

"He's never said any of that to me," I answered, a little testy.

"Maybe he doesn't know how."

One day Jimmy phoned to ask if I wanted to go bowling.

Was this a *date?* It didn't feel like it. More like the kind of palling around we had been doing.

Then a numbing thought struck me. What if Jimmy wouldn't ask me out? What if he just kept casually phoning and hanging out? What if even Jimmy with the funny clothes and big shoes wasn't interested in me?

After bowling he took me home. He parked in front of my house in his father's beat-up old Falcon but didn't make a move to get out. Instead he put his arm on the top of the car seat and asked, "Listen, how about a date this Saturday night? We could go to the movies in Salinas."

All I heard was *date!*

That afternoon I waited anxiously for my mother to come home after working the swing shift from 7:00 a.m. to 4:00 p.m.

"Mamá, he asked me to the movies," I exclaimed as soon as she crossed the doorway.

"*Sí?* How nice! But, *mi'ja,* for an evening date you must ask your father's permission." She smiled and gave me a hug.

Dinner was interminable. I could barely swallow the food and when I did it stuck in my throat before winding its way to my knotted stomach. I shifted back and forth in my chair, waiting to find the proper timing to jump in the conversation and make my request. I shouldn't do it while he was eating, but then again, I shouldn't wait until he left the table. Timing was very important in dealing with my cranky stepfather; the right mood and the right moment made the difference between a week of sullen silence or good humor. My mother attributed his mood swings to his diabetes. I wasn't so sure.

I watched Papá's face carefully, noting every facial nuance, muscle twitch, and change of expression. He seemed in a genial mood, talking about how good the tomato crops were and about the work he was doing on the farm. I waited patiently until there was a lull in the conversation. Taking a deep breath, I exhaled, letting my words come out in a gush of air. His relaxed features suddenly hardened and his mouth grew tight.

"No. Only American *putas* go out alone with men."

His words took the wind out of me. Tears stung my eyes.

My mother was just as surprised. I knew she had not expected this reaction or else she wouldn't have set me up like this.

"You don't have the right to talk like that to her, old man. She has a nice *pretendiente*. I know his mother," she explained.

"In Mexico, only whores go out with men without chaperones..."

"*¡No estamos en México, viejo!*" my mother said.

"My sisters met their boyfriends on the corner of the street and didn't disgrace our family home," he said, ignoring her words.

"And you think standing on corners is better than inviting someone into your own home?" My mother's tone of voice was ironic. It was unspoken but understood that her family came from a higher social class than his. Their differences in backgrounds surfaced during arguments. I glanced at him and immediately realized he would handle this situation just like all the other times. His face turned granite, immovable, unyielding, and silent.

"You're wrong this time," my mother said in an even voice, although I saw her chin quiver and her eyes glisten. She turned on her heel and vanished into the kitchen. I hastily retreated into my room and turned up the radio as high as I could.

Papá stopped talking to us and we to him. Meals were placed on the table for him but no one said a word. I stayed out of his way, mostly in my room.

Mamá insisted I keep my date with Jimmy.

For the next few days my attention was spent agonizing on what to wear Saturday night. Jeans? A dress? A skirt? There was no one to ask. No one I wanted to admit to that I didn't know what to wear on a date to dinner and movies, that is. I chose the lime green mini-dress I'd worn to my senior awards day and threw a white sweater around my shoulders.

Jimmy arrived promptly. He stood on the other side of the screen door, waiting to be invited in. His mouth was twisted in a small smile that made him look tense and unsure.

This is what he saw: my scowling father staring into a TV blaring in Spanish; my overly friendly mother, waving and gushing simultaneously; and me, grinning grimly. One of our expressions—God knows whose—encouraged him to try to open the door, but it was locked. His smile faded. Nobody made a move to welcome him in. My mother gently nudged me forward. I quickly hugged and kissed her, ignored Papá like he was doing with me, and walked out.

"Whew! What's going on in there?" Jimmy asked once inside the car. "I didn't think you were going to make it out!"

I waved my hand dismissively. How could I possibly explain when I didn't understand the situation myself?

He didn't pursue the question. In fact, Jimmy didn't say much. I thought he would say I looked nice or that he liked my dress. That's how first dates in the movies started. I couldn't help noticing he was wearing yet another outfit from the time-warp zone.

"You know, I feel a little bad because I don't know the latest good restaurants," he finally said apologetically. "Too much has changed and gone out of style since I've been gone."

"Yeah, like clothes," I thought unkindly. I was annoyed he hadn't thought to ask about a good restaurant.

"You like Chinese? There's this place I used to go to when I was in school. You wanna try it?"

"Sure, why not?" I said.

I observed him more closely and saw that his hair seemed a little longer tonight. His olive skin shone smooth and well scrubbed. Even the tips of his ears were pink. I caught a whiff of Jade East cologne. It smelled nice and subtle, not like the boys at school dances who reeked as if they had poured the whole bottle on themselves.

The restaurant was in the old part of downtown Salinas. Ever since Monte Mart had been opened in Alisal and new strip malls and a shopping center were being built in North Salinas, this part of town had become rundown and practically deserted. Many buildings were boarded up. Only a few cheap stores and restaurants like the one we were walking into remained. Inside, the sparse dining room was furnished with Formica tables and flowered vinyl chairs. Faded plastic flowers were stuck haphazardly in milk-glass vases.

"Maybe the food's still good," Jimmy said, winking at me.

We both laughed, the tension between us dissolved. Conversation flowed easily after that. Jimmy leaned toward me across the table, his eyes soft and playful, his face relaxed. He was the most talkative since I'd met him.

I was curious about his experiences in Vietnam but the right opportunity to ask him had not presented itself. Now—warmed by the meal, drinking hot tea, a comfortable conversation fanning a spark between us—it seemed like the right time.

"You hear a lot of things about Vietnam and see stuff on the news every night, but you were there..." I hesitated.

A flash of emotion crossed his face but he quickly shrugged it off.

"The toughest thing is losing a buddy. One day you're training with him, joking and sharing cigarettes, talking about girls. Then you get shipped off—one of you goes to fight and the other one goes to a desk job." He shook his head sadly, "And, you know, everybody says it's God's will what happens. But it's not. It's just the luck of the draw."

"Well, that's the same thing, isn't it? Fate is up to God," I said softly.

He looked at me funny and said coldly, "No. Just some damn clerk."

He made me feel like I'd said the stupidest thing in the world.

Outside, the sea breeze from Monterey blew cold fog into the Salinas night. Jimmy grabbed his military jacket before going into the theater and I regretted having worn a dress. A beefy man with short blond hair standing behind us in line tapped Jimmy on the shoulder and said, "Excuse me, son. I just want to tell you that you boys are doing a real good job for our country."

Jimmy thanked him politely but I noticed his face remained blank.

I don't recall what movie we saw. I do recall his arm around my shoulder and an attempt at a kiss that was so awkward he didn't try again.

By the time we got out of the theater the night felt frigid. The evening fog's icy fingers poked through my thin sweater. I shivered. Jimmy looked cozy in his big green jacket.

"Hey, Johnnie! How many boys did you kill for Uncle Sam?" The jeers came from across the street. Long-haired boys probably around my age chortled in the shadows.

I couldn't see Jimmy's face, just his profile, and that offered no clue to his feelings. He said nothing. I thought I should say something, touch his arm, to offer some reassurance. But once again the right response evaded me.

Silence hung over us like a cloud as we drove through the dark stretch of country road through the Salinas Valley. No moonlight illuminated the fields and the eucalyptus trees that shielded the crops from wind.

We made small talk about the movie and other movies we'd seen. He liked James Bond, I liked *Love Story*.

"*Love Story?* God! That was so sappy!" Jimmy grimaced.

I searched for a different topic. "Do you have a favorite book or author?"

"Nah. I can't tell you about the books I've been reading lately!" he said, raising his eyebrows for emphasis.

"Well, I really like the Brontë sisters."

He yawned audibly.

"Do you like the Giants?"

Jimmy's eyes lit up. "Are you kidding? I'd kill to see a game at the 'Stick! Are you a fan too?"

Of course I wasn't, but at least his sports prattle bridged the silence that lapsed between us.

When we got to my house, the light glowing on the front porch was the only thing visible on the street. There were no street lamps on my side of town. Outside the air felt warm, unlike the cold in Salinas.

We walked quietly up to my front door. I turned toward him to thank him for the evening, but before I could utter a sound, he took my face in his hands and kissed me gently, sweetly. I kissed him back.

He stood back blinking and said, "Wow. After the movie, I thought maybe you didn't really want to kiss me."

We kissed again. I gave him a smile and quickly let myself into the house. I heard a stumble outside, then the sound of feet crunching on gravel as they walked away from the house. The car engine ignited, followed by the squeal of wheels turning down the street, and then stillness.

My back leaned heavily against the door. I closed my eyes. My heart fluttered in my chest like a bird against a window pane. I waited. I heard no music, no bells or the rush of warmth described in novels. I felt nothing at all.

27

THE CONVEYOR BELT LADIES

THE CONVEYOR BELT LADIES WERE MIGRANT WOMEN, mostly from Texas. I worked with them during the summers of my teenage years. I call them conveyor belt ladies because I got to know them while sorting tomatoes on a conveyor belt.

The women and their families arrived in May for the carrot season, spent the summer in the tomato sheds, and stayed through October for the bean harvest. After that, they emptied from town, some returning to their homes in Texas while others continued on the migrant trail, picking cotton in the San Joaquin Valley or grapefruits and oranges in the Imperial Valley.

Most of these women had started in the fields. The vegetable packing sheds were a step up, easier than the backbreaking jobs in the fields. The work in the sheds was often more tedious than strenuous, paid better, and provided fairly steady hours and clean bathrooms. Best of all, you didn't get rained on.

I had started sorting tomatoes with my mother in high school. I would have preferred working in a dress shop or babysitting like my friends, but I had a dream that would cost a lot of money—college—and the fact was that sorting tomatoes was the highest-paying work in town. The job consisted of picking out the flawed tomatoes on the conveyor belt before they rolled into the shipping boxes at the end of the line. These boxes were immediately loaded onto delivery trucks, so it was important not to let bad tomatoes through.

The work could be slow or intense, depending on the quality of the tomatoes and how many there were. Work increased when the company deliveries got backlogged or after rain delayed picking. During those times, it was not unusual to work from 7:00 a.m. until midnight. I never heard anyone complain about overtime, though. Overtime meant desperately needed extra money.

It would have been difficult not to like the women. They were an entertaining group, easing the long, monotonous hours with bawdy humor and spicy gossip. They poked fun at all the male workers and did hysterical impersonations of the supervisor. Although he didn't speak Spanish (other than *"¡Mujeres, trabajo, trabajo!* Women, work, work!"), he sensed he was being laughed at. He would stamp his foot and forbid us from talking until break time. But it would have been much easier to tie the women's tongues in knots than to keep them quiet. Eventually the ladies had their way and their fun, and the men learned to ignore them.

Pretty Rosa described her romances and her pending wedding to a handsome fieldworker. Berta told me that Rosa's marriage would cause her nothing but headaches because the man was younger and too handsome. María, large and placid, described the births of each of her nine children, warning me about the horrors of labor and delivery.

At other moments they could turn melancholic, telling of babies who died because their mothers couldn't afford medical care, the alcoholic husbands who were their "cross to bear," the racism they experienced in Texas, where they were referred to as "dirty Mexicans" or "Mexican dogs" and not allowed in certain restaurants.

I was appalled and deeply moved by these confidences, and the injustices they endured enraged me. I could do little but sympathize. My mother, no stranger to suffering, said I was too impressionable when I emotionally relayed to her the women's stories.

"If they were in Mexico, life would be even harder. At least there are opportunities here; you can work," she'd say.

During that first summer, I learned to respect the conveyor belt ladies.

The last summer I worked in the packing shed turned out to be the last I lived at home. I had just finished junior college and was transferring to a university. At this point I was "overeducated" for seasonal work, but if you counted the overtime, it was still the best-paying job. So I went back one last time.

The ladies treated me with warmth and respect. I was a college student and they thought I deserved special treatment.

Aguedita, the crew chief, moved me to softer and better-paying jobs within the plant. I moved from the conveyor belt to shoving boxes down a chute and finally to weighing boxes of tomatoes on a scale—the highest-paying position for a woman.

When the union representative showed up to collect dues, the women hid me in the bathroom. They had determined it was unfair for me to have to pay dues since I worked only during the summer. We played a cat-and-mouse game with him all summer. "You ladies aren't hiding students, are you?" he'd ask suspiciously.

"Why does *la unión* charge our poor students anyway?" The ladies would distract him with questions and complaints until he tired of answering them and had to leave for his next location.

María, with the nine children, tried to feed me all summer, bringing extra tortillas, which were delicious. I accepted them with some guilt, wondering if I was taking food away from her children. Others brought rental contracts or other documents for me to explain and translate.

The last day of work was splendidly beautiful, golden and warm. The conveyor belt's loud humming was turned off, silenced for the season. The women sighed as they removed their aprons. Some of them walked off, calling, "*¡Hasta la próxima!* Until next time!"

But most of the conveyor belt ladies came over to me, shook my hand, and gave me a blessing or a big hug.

"Don't come back. Make us proud, *hija.*"

About the Author

Rose Castillo Guilbault left her home in King City to attend Palomar College in San Diego County, where she was editor of the school newspaper. After receiving her A.A. from Palomar, she enrolled at San Jose State University, where she graduated with a B.A. in broadcast journalism. Later, she also earned an M.B.A. from Pepperdine University and an M.A. in writing from the University of San Francisco.

Guilbault began her broadcasting career at the CBS television affiliate in San Francisco, where she produced documentaries and public affairs programs, winning an Emmy Award for outstanding children's programming. Later, she joined the ABC television affiliate, where she became well known to Northern California audiences for her on-air editorials and pioneering work in local programming, including producing primetime specials highlighting diverse communities. She is currently the vice president of corporate affairs at AAA of Northern California, Nevada, and Utah.

Guilbault has been a community activist her entire professional life. She was the only journalist on President George H. W. Bush's Advisory Commission on Education Excellence for Hispanic Americans, and she has received many awards for her service on behalf of other organizations in the community, among them the Simon Bolivar Award from the Hispanic Community Foundation, the Eleanor Roosevelt Humanitarian Award from the San Francisco United Nations Association, and the "A Woman Who Could Be President" Award from the League of Women Voters. She has been involved with the

Commonwealth Club of California for more than a decade and currently heads their Board of Governors as the first Latina chairwoman in the organization's century-long history.

Guilbault's essays have been published in more than one hundred educational books, anthologies, readers, and textbooks, and her writing was syndicated for a number of years by the Pacific News Service. This memoir grew out of a column Guilbault wrote for the *San Francisco Chronicle* from 1989 to 1991 called "Hispanic, USA."

Guilbault has been married for thirty years to her college sweetheart and they have two daughters. The couple lives in the San Francisco Bay Area.

Acknowledgments

Many people have influenced, inspired, supported, and helped with the writings in this book. Richard Rodriguez "discovered" me as a writer and has been a great mentor. I owe Sandy Close at the Pacific News Service a great deal of gratitude for nurturing my writing, editing original versions of some of the stories included in this book, and being a dear friend. I also want to thank Lyle York, former editor for the *San Francisco Chronicle,* who hired me to be the paper's first columnist to write about Hispanic issues. I am grateful to two friends whose confidence in my writing buoyed me through storms of doubt: Beverly Hayon, whose encouragement has been constant, and the late, great José Antonio Burciaga. Tony Burciaga encouraged and admired my writing and, by example, demonstrated it was possible to tell our stories the way we wanted to tell them. I miss his creative spirit and his wise presence.

Thanks also to the staff at Heyday Books, who are a pleasure to work with: Jeannine Gendar, Lisa K. Manwill, Zak Nelson, Katie Wadell, Rebecca LeGates, and Lorraine Rath, as well as publishing icon Malcolm Margolin, who is brilliant.

I am forever indebted to my late parents, María Luisa Corral Rábago de García and my stepfather José Celedonío García Inclan, who lived their lives with dignity, faith, and optimism for a better future. And to my daughters, Natalie and Jacquie, who carry the gift of storytelling. I hope they honor this family legacy by passing it on to their own generations.

And last but hardly least, my most significant influence: my husband, Richard, who is the guiding light and force behind this publication. His determination in making this project a reality and his faith in my writing are but two examples of his love and generosity. May my daughters be so lucky as to marry men like their father.

GLOSSARY

adiós: good-bye

los americanos: the Americans

ándale: hurry up

Ave María Purísima: a call to the Virgin Mary

a ver, niña: let's see, little girl

buñuelos: fried flour tortillas topped with sugar or syrup and
    served with dessert

campesinos: farmworkers

cariño: gift

casa chica: little house

casa grande: big house

Castellanos: people of Spanish heritage

Chapayekas: figures costumed to represent evil spirits and
    temptation

charreadas: rodeos

Chavistas: supporters of César Chávez; members of his farm
    workers union

china poblana: a style of ethnic dress commonly worn by dancers
    performing the Mexican hat dance

chubasco: heavy rainstorm

churros: long strips of fried dough covered with cinnamon
    and sugar

claro que si: of course

comadres: best women friends

comal: a large cast-iron plate used to make tortillas

con sacrificios: with sacrifices

Cristeros: Catholic rebels believed to have buried precious
    religious objects to protect them from government troops

cuidado: be careful

cuídate: look after yourself

déjala: leave her alone; forget it

Dios mío: my God

empanaditas: small empanadas

envidias: jealousies

época del oro: the "golden era" of Mexican cinema, during the
  thirties and forties

ese hombre: that guy

los Estados Unidos: the United States

estás loca: you are crazy

estas ollas, serán "pots" en inglés?: these pots, are they "pots" in
  English?

el Gachupín: a slightly derogatory term for a Spaniard

gente chismosa: gossips

gente decente: decent people

gringa/o: slightly derogatory term for an American

güera: light-skinned

hermana/o: sister/brother

hija: daughter

hijo de su madre: son of a bitch

hola: hello

hombre: man

hombre sinvergüenza: scoundrel

huelguistas: union strikers

huevón: a vulgar term for a lazy person

importante: important

inglés: English

latillas: small sticks used to cover ceilings

Licha: nickname for María Luisa

malagradecida: ingrate

masa: dough

Matachines: costumed dancers appearing in religious festivals
  and parades

menudo: soup cooked for celebrations that is also believed to
   cure hangovers
metiches: pests
mi'ja: my daughter
mi'jita: my little daughter
mira: look
misa de gallo: midnight mass; literally "mass of the rooster"
muy romántico: very romantic
nalgas: buttocks
negro: black; dark-skinned
niña: girl
ni uno: not one
no estamos en México, viejo: we are not in Mexico, old man
no hay comida: you don't have any food
nopal: cactus; can also refer to cactus paddles, which are eaten in
a variety of ways
novelas: television soap operas
novios: boyfriends
panocha: brown sugar
Pascola: the host of the fiesta
piojos: lice
piropos: compliments, passes
pobrecitos: poor things
pobre diablo: poor devil
posadas: reenactments through processions and songs about
   Joseph and Mary's seeking shelter in Bethlehem; generally
   organized in a neighborhood where participants go door to
   door until the last household lets everyone in and they
   celebrate with food, drinks, and games
pretendiente: suitor
prima americana: American cousin
profesional: professional
pueblo: village
pues: of course you can
putas: whores

que Dios te bendiga: may God bless you

qué lástima: what a pity

quién sabe: who knows

quizá: perhaps

ranchero music: a unique style of music, usually featuring accordions and guitars, associated with rural Mexico

rancho: farm

rompope: Mexican eggnog

señor/a: sir/ma'am

sí: yes

simón: yeah

sociedad: society

solterona: spinster

tiendita: small store selling staples

los Tres Reyes Magos: the Three Wise Men, who are celebrated on January 6; children leave their shoes outside their rooms and awake to find them filled with candy, fruit, and toys

viejitas: little old ladies

viejo: old man

vigas: rafters

Yaquis: Indian people native to northern Mexico

zócalo: main square; plaza where people can stroll, socialize, and hold concerts